José Jailton Junior
Tássio Costa

Integration of Heterogeneous Wireless Networks to Compose 5G Networks

José Jailton Junior
Tássio Costa

Integration of Heterogeneous Wireless Networks to Compose 5G Networks

Connectivity for Smart Cities

ScienciaScripts

Imprint

Any brand names and product names mentioned in this book are subject to trademark, brand or patent protection and are trademarks or registered trademarks of their respective holders. The use of brand names, product names, common names, trade names, product descriptions etc. even without a particular marking in this work is in no way to be construed to mean that such names may be regarded as unrestricted in respect of trademark and brand protection legislation and could thus be used by anyone.

Cover image: www.ingimage.com

This book is a translation from the original published under ISBN 978-613-9-69738-0.

Publisher:
Sciencia Scripts
is a trademark of
Dodo Books Indian Ocean Ltd. and OmniScriptum S.R.L publishing group

120 High Road, East Finchley, London, N2 9ED, United Kingdom
Str. Armeneasca 28/1, office 1, Chisinau MD-2012, Republic of Moldova, Europe
Printed at: see last page
ISBN: 978-620-8-13888-2

Contents

CHAPTER 1

Introduction

1.1 Overview

In the context of research, interoperability and integration between heterogeneous wireless technologies is a challenge that, when overcome, will allow users to have various connectivity opportunities and enjoy the best service and wireless access for their context. Therefore, a fundamental aspect for the design of the so-called Fifth Generation Networks is the development of architectures that enable both transparent mobility and adequate support for QoS (Quality of Service) for applications in this ubiquitous communications scenario made up of heterogeneous and wireless technologies.

The current trend also points to the popularisation of portable devices equipped with multiple interfaces (multimodal terminals) of heterogeneous wireless technologies, such as WiFi (Wireless Fidelity), WiMAX (Worldwide Interoperability for Microwave Access), 3G/UMTS (Universal Mobile Telecommunications System) and LTE (Long Term Evolution). This is already a reality, for example, for mobile phones that allow the user 5G, 4G, 3G, WiFi, Bluetooth connectivity, generally through manual switching between these technologies. In these heterogeneous networks, access should be transparent and, preferably, the user should always be connected to the best network (ABC - Always Best Connectivity) (AOYAMA, 2009; ET, 2011).

Mobile devices have become an essential part of our daily lives and, as such, the mobile network infrastructure that connects them has become critical. Fifth Generation (5G) mobile systems will support a wide range of services and devices (ASTELY et ah, 2009). 5G is being designed to be a multi-service network that supports a diverse set of performance and service requirements. And indeed, 5G will be a paradigm shift that includes carrier frequencies, bandwidth,
connectivity between base station and mobile devices and even quantities of antennas. But unlike the previous four generations, it will also be highly integrative: interconnecting different technologies (e.g. LTE and Wi-Fi) to provide universal high-rate coverage and a seamless user experience. To support this, the core network will also have to achieve unprecedented levels of flexibility and intelligence, spectrum regulation will need to be rethought and improved, and energy and cost efficiency will become even more critical factors.

Heterogeneous networks are being widely studied and different solutions are being proposed by research groups. Numerous initiatives related to the implementation of projects using heterogeneous Mesh networks have been carried out (MESHNET, 2007).

The term Smart City refers to the ability to offer connectivity to mobile users, the main connection link being via the Base Stations (BS) scattered around the city, but this would not be the only form of connection that can be extended to users via Access Points. Electricity poles can serve as Access Points, telephone exchanges, buildings and even vehicles can be used.

Figure 1 exemplifies the concept of Smart Cities with the integration of Heterogeneous Networks using mesh communication.

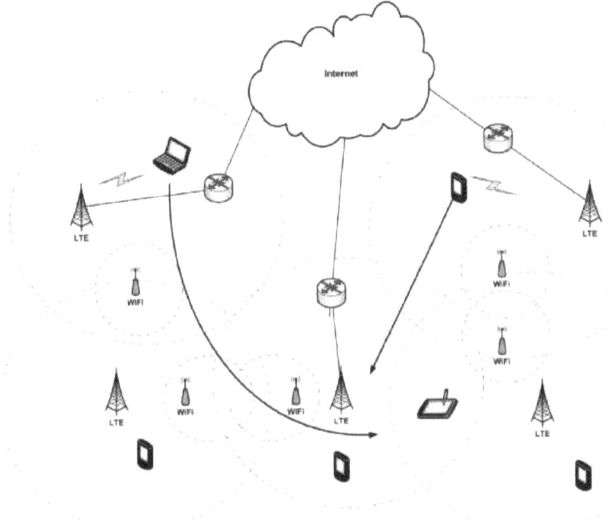

Figure 1: Integration of Heterogeneous Networks

Source: Author

Currently, communication network technologies are gaining more and more ground in the market as well as in research. Specifically, wireless networks provide the main characteristics required: high data transfer rates and mobility, respectively. However, until now, these technologies that support the various activities in the area of ICT (Information and Communication Technology) have been viewed independently, which does not exploit all the multiplier potential that can be realised with their integration and interoperability.

A major advance involves the use of these networks in mesh mode, where a mobile device can be a potential router, extending network coverage according to a wireless multi-hop routing model. Wireless mesh networks (AKYILDIZ; WANG; WANG, 2005) have emerged in recent years as facilitators in the process of digital inclusion. Mesh technology enables computers and networks to connect to the Internet via multiple wireless hops, eliminating the need for cables, like any wireless network, but allowing wireless network coverage to be extended beyond the traditional limits of a single hop.

Although wireless mesh networks operate in ad hoc mode, which is also used by other types of wireless networks, they bring new characteristics that differentiate them from the latter and therefore require new protocols and functions with different requirements from those used by traditional ad hoc wireless network architectures (AKYILDIZ; WANG; WANG, 2005). One important function, for which the research community has not yet reached a consensus, is routing, i.e. how a client node determines the best path to reach the gateway node that provides access to the Internet considering the availability of several wireless hops between the client and the gateway. These wireless hops can pass through mobile routers, and the quality characteristics of the links connecting the routers can vary greatly. Hence the need to re-evaluate traditional ad hoc routing protocols so that mesh networks can exploit their full connectivity potential.

The challenges facing the 5ª Generation Network have prompted a lot of research into providing users with transparent and ubiquitous access to services. When the handover occurs between cells of the same technology, the procedure is called a horizontal handover, as in the case of a client who is being served by a Base Station (BS) and who, due to mobility or a drop in signal quality, is now served by a new BS of the same technology. On the other hand, when the cell change procedure takes place between different technologies, for example between WLAN (Wireless Local Area Network) and WMAN (Wireless Metropolitan Area Network), the procedure is called vertical handover (ASTELY et ah, 2009; ANAS et ah, 2007).

In the context of integrating heterogeneous architectures, Vehicular Ad Hoc Networks (VANETs) have emerged as a potential connectivity technology aimed at the user experience, since their implementation typically comprises various communication technologies, including Dedicated Short-range Communication (DSRC), Wi-Fi, 4G and 5G (YAQOOB et ah, 2017).

On the other hand, the study of vehicular networks is also motivated by recent advances in artificial intelligence and sensor technologies, autonomous or self-driving vehicles that are able to sense their surroundings in real time by the combined use of many techniques, including radar, GPS. Consequently, the autonomous vehicle is closer to reality than we think (YAQOOB et al., 2017). However, it is unlikely that fully autonomous vehicles (AVs) will be commercially available before 2020, but once the technological and regulatory issues are resolved, it is estimated that up to 15 per cent of new cars sold in 2030 could be fully autonomous according to the survey (MOHR et al., 2016). Research shows that Americans alone spend more than 500 million working hours a week in their cars, and that number continues to rise. Thus, vehicles have become an important part of people's mobile experience (ZHANG; BAI; JU, 2015). Knowing this, connectivity and, later, autonomous technology, will increasingly allow the car to become a platform for drivers and passengers to use their transit time for personal activities, which can include the use of new forms of media and services (MOHR et al., 2016).

Connectivity in VANETs is achieved through vehicle-to-vehicle (V2V) or vehicle-to-infrastructure (V2I) communications. In V2V, vehicles communicate with each other on an ad hoc basis, while in V2I, vehicles connect with pre-existing infrastructure on the sides of the road, which are often referred to as Road Side Units (RSU). V2V communication is often a challenge due to the high mobility of vehicles, which does not allow for stable connections between them, while V2I generally results in a high cost of installation and maintenance. RSUs are considered the backbone of V2I messaging and are connected to provide connectivity to vehicles.

Effective mobility management, specifically handover (changing the channel, AP or BS as the user moves or suffers degradation in signal quality), is extremely important and fundamental to the success of new applications and, consequently, of these networks. With the advance of mobile computing and the popularisation of smartphones, new wireless network architectures must provide a heterogeneous connectivity environment. By providing users with alternative connections, users will be able to choose the technology according to their needs at the time.

Users of mobile devices with multiple interfaces will be able to handover between heterogeneous wireless technologies. This gives rise to a new concept of connectivity that makes mobility management more complex, since a user can change technology (as long as they are in a coverage area) with a higher or lower transmission rate depending on their needs. This is why it is necessary to develop an algorithm that allows continuity of services even during the transition period between technologies.

It is desirable for connection selection to be automatic, without user intervention. The purpose of automatic technology selection is to guarantee the quality of service to the user. For example, in situations where the user is connected to a network with low data transmission and detects the presence of a network with better transmission parameters, the mobile device itself would make the network change transparently without causing damage to the quality of service (without breaking the connection). There is therefore a need to develop an algorithm capable of evaluating the network parameters of different technologies (signal strength, transmission rate) so that it can select the best network according to the circumstances at the time and the user's profile.

The following chapters will describe each of these architectures (LTE, Mesh Networks and Vehicular Networks) that will be important for the composition of a mobile system for 5G Networks. The simulator used in the research to carry out the simulations was Network Simulator 3 (NS-3) in version 3.25, which is a discrete event simulation tool for Internet systems (NETWORK SIMULATOR 3, 2016), and is widely used by the international scientific research community in computer networks. The simulator's main difference and advantage is that it offers a mass of models of different technologies available for simulations, especially models of wireless systems and a variety of protocols.

CHAPTER 2

LTE networks

Author: Henrique Júnior Jaques Pereira[1]

2.1   Overview

This chapter looks at the history of fourth generation networks, especially LTE (Long Term Evolution) technology, with an emphasis on its beginnings, evolution and operation. The main components and subsystems will also be presented, as well as the auxiliary technologies that make up the 4G/LTE network.

There will also be an explanation of the handover procedure, which is common in cellular networks, especially in the LTE network. Simulation results of an LTE network exposed to different possible realistic scenarios, carried out in the Network Simulator 3 simulator, will also be presented.

2.2   Emergence of the LTE Network

Due to the constant and growing need to develop means of obtaining large volumes of data, mobile networks need to evolve. The large amount of information travelling over cellular networks (2G, EDGE, 3G, HSPA) and the Internet, through downloads and uploads, is due to the increase in the number of users of mobile devices connected to these technologies. For this reason, there is a constant search for new technologies to support fast, secure and efficient information retrieval.

The Long Term Evolution (LTE) network, standardised by 3GPP, is a fourth-generation mobile telephony technology, which differs from other technologies in that it provides faster data traffic and greater bandwidth.

Worldwide Interoperability for Microwave Access (WiMax) is a technology that also belongs to the fourth generation of mobile telephony. According to (AOYAMA, 2009), WiMax can work in point or multipoint mode, eliminating the need for wires and is capable of providing up to 10 Mbps. The main difference between LTE and WiMax technologies is that the former is compatible with the resources present in HSPA and GSM networks, enabling mobile devices to make the transition to LTE without service discontinuity.

The LTE standard was publicly tested in 2009 in Sweden, and in the United States it was

---

[1]Master's student in Computer Science, UFPE, Computer Centre, E-mail: hjjp@cin.ufpe.br

trialled in 2010. The technology is still being deployed around the world and represents an important moment in the field of telecommunications, where users are no longer accepting a lower transmission bandwidth in exchange for greater mobility, as was the case in previous generations, but are demanding both in their devices. In Brazil, the LTE standard began to be deployed in 2012 when ANATEL put the 2500 MHz frequency band out to tender, and is adopted as the main 4G technology by the country's four largest telephone companies (TIM, VIVO, OI and CLARO). Figure 2 shows a table with the number of mobile phones with a 4G connection in Brazil.

	Jun/16	Dec/16	May/17	Jun/17
4G mobile phones	39702	60 104	76.334	80.560
Density	19.3	29.1	36,8	33.8
	2 343	3.998	2.276	4 226
Growth Month	6.3%	7,1%	3,1%	5,5%
	14255	34 658	16.230	20 456
Growth Year	56,0%	136,2%	27,0%	34,0%
	26 537	34.658	38.981	40.859
Growth in 1 year	201.6%	136,2%	104,4%	102,9%

Figure 2: Mobile phones with 4G technology in Brazil from Jun/2016 to Jun/2017

Source: (TELECO, 2018a)

1.3 LTE Network Features

Listed below are some of the characteristics that differentiate the LTE network from other mobile networks:

- Because it supports several network bands, regardless of their frequency, it can operate in conjunction with other networks;

-Reduced network latency;

-Peak speeds can reach up to 300 Mbps downlink and 75 Mbps uplink;

-Compared to previous technologies, LTE has little impact on the data transmission rate when the user is on the move.

The technology's main effort is to minimise the complexity of the system and user equipment, as well as allowing flexible spectral distribution across new frequencies (a subject that will be covered later). The technology is designed to support IP-based data traffic with quality of service.

2.4 Architecture Components

At a macroscopic level, the LTE network is basically made up of a base station, end terminals, the PGW component and the addition of the Internet, as shown in Figure 23.

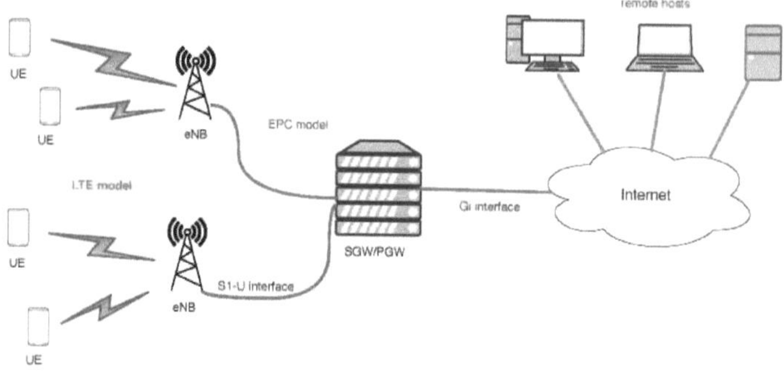

Figure 3: Macroscopic View of an LTE Architecture

Adapted from: (NETWORK SIMULATOR 3, 2016)

According to (D'AVILA, 2009), the differences that distinguish the LTE network from previous generation networks are the exclusion of the RNC (Radio Network Controller) and the IP-based system. Figure 4 outlines the components and their relationships of the LTE standard architecture at a more detailed level.

The network has four main domains:

- User Equipament (UE): User access device.

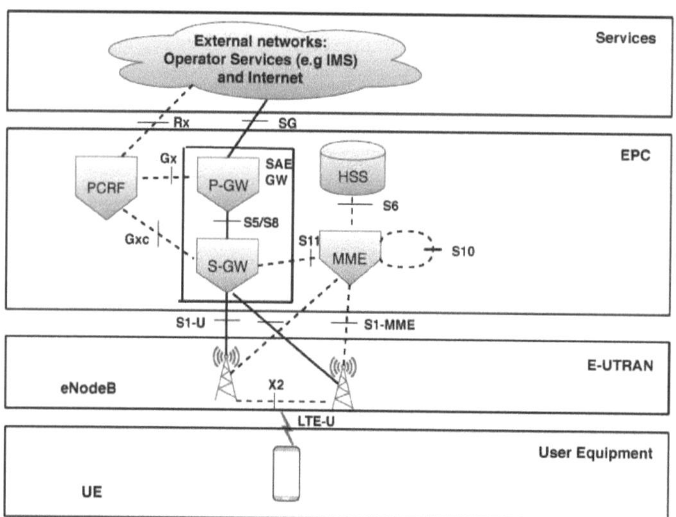

Figura 4:   Internal LTE Network Architecture

Adapted from: (TELECO, 2018b)

- eNodeB/Base Station (eNB): Tower responsible for providing a connection to the UE. The eNodeB covers the physical (PHY), Medium Access Control (MAC), Radio Link Control (RLC) and packet data control protocol layers. It also includes header compression, encryption, radio resource management, admission control, quality of service negotiation and uplink functionality.

- E-UTRAN: Introduced by 3GPP R8, it is the LTE network path area interface consisting of a web of eNBs that communicate via the X2 interface. Its purpose is to replace the UMTS and HSDPA/HSUPA technologies specified in the 3GPP R5 version.

- Evolved Packet Core (EPC): This contains the main network elements allowing integration with other communication networks based on the IP protocol, using packet switching. Its subsystems carry out the system's main tasks and are defined as:

Mobile Management Entity (MME): This is responsible for user mobility and for signalling and authentication, security, establishing connections and authorising services, among other things. It is also responsible for idle mode, i.e. when no connections have yet been established with any carrier. In other words, it is the substantial control element in the EPC.

Serving Gateway (S-GW): This is responsible for routing user IP packets between the LTE network and other technologies such as 2G, 3G and the Internet, guaranteeing network interoperability. In addition, the S-GW has control and air-

storage of UE information, interpreting it as parameters of supported IP services.

Packet Data Network Gateway (P-GW): This is the edge router between the EPC and external packet networks.

Policy and Charging Rules Function (PCRF): Provides support for service data flow detection, i.e. it provides a load control and quality of service policy so that the requested services can make use of the appropriate resources.

Home Subscriber Server (HSS): This is responsible for storing and updating when necessary the database containing all the user's subscription information.

Service Layer: realises the interoperability of the LTE network with other external networks.

1.5   LTE Technology Operation

The LTE standard emerged from the improvement of the UMTS telecommunications network through E-UTRAN and is followed by the evolution of terms that are part of systems architecture evolution (SAE). These technologies belong to the evolved packet system (EPS).

Within the LTE network, the UE connects to an eNodeB (which can support around 400 simultaneously connected users), which will be responsible for carrying out information processing tasks, as well as controlling data traffic, ensuring the quality of the service provided. This is followed by user authentication, service provision authorisation and control signalling in the MIME subsystem. Sequentially, the HSS server is activated to provide control information for the MIME and store information about the user.

Once the UE has successfully authenticated itself on the network and started data traffic, the

S-GW is called to route the data packets between the LTE network and external networks, such as the Internet. After this process, the PCRF is called to manage the service policy, as well as sending quality of service configuration information. The P-GW is put into operation as an edge router, i.e. it will act as the interface for the EPC core's data path with external data networks. Finally, with interoperability guaranteed by the subsystems of the EPC core, data transmission services will be realised between the LTE network and the Internet, for example.

2.6The   Protocol Stack of the LTE Standard

Understanding the entire operating mode of the LTE network in its smallest details is not a trivial task. In addition to all the complexity present in its subsystems, especially in the EPC core, there is also a set of protocols responsible for intercommunication between the subsystems and for conducting information through the communication media. The most important network protocols will be described below, as well as the function of each one. Figure 5 shows the layout of the LTE network's protocol stack.

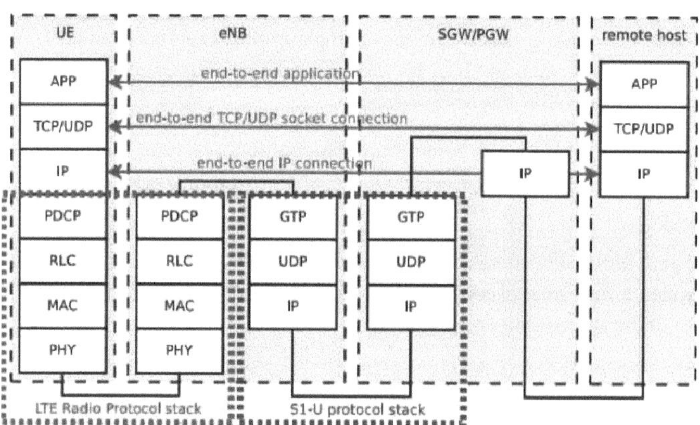

Figura 5:   LTE Network Protocol Stack

Source: (NETWORK SIMULATOR 3, 2016)

- Radio Resource Control (RRC): eNB makes decisions to trigger the handover process based on measurements of the signal level of neighbouring towers that are collected by the UE. In addition, this protocol sends broadcast messages containing system information and controls measurements of UE parameters.

- Packet Data Control Protocol (PDCP): This protocol is responsible for compressing and decompressing IP packet headers using Robust Header Compression (ROHC). This function enables efficient bandwidth utilisation on the air interface.

- Radio Link Control (RLC): This is the protocol responsible for segmentation, concatenation, retransmission handling and delivery of data in sequence to the upper layers. In general terms, RLC is used to format and transport data between the UE and the eNB.

- Medium Access Control (MAC): This is responsible for mapping logical channels to transport channels. The MAC layer provides services to the RLC via logical channels.

-PHY   : Protocol that acts at the physical layer of the LTE network. It transports information from higher layers.

2.7 Frequency Bands and Transmission Rates Operated by LTE

Around the world, telephone operators using the LTE network can use various frequency bands, which are standardised by the E-UTRA specification. In Brazil, for example, operators use E-UTRA band number seven, in the 2.5 GHz band, while in the United States they use bands 12, 13, 14, 17 and 29, which are in the 700 MHz band.

To better understand the frequency bands in which the network can operate, it is necessary to understand the concept of FDD (Frequency Division Duplex) and TDD (Time Division Duplex). According to (ASTELY et al., 2009), time division duplexing (TDD) uses time to provide a direct link and a reverse link, i.e. several users share the same channel alternating only time. Frequency division duplexing (FDD), on the other hand, provides two separate frequency bands for each user. The forward band provides traffic from the eNB to the UE, and the reverse band provides traffic from the UE to the eNB. Figure 6 shows the table with the operating frequency bands outlined by 3GPP.

FDD

Banda	Frequências UL/DL (MHz)
1	1920 - 1980 / 2110 - 2170
2	1850 - 1910 / 1930 - 1990
3	1710 - 1785 / 1805 - 1880
4	1710 - 1755 / 2110 - 2155
5	824 - 849 / 869 - 894
6	830 - 840 / 875 - 885
7	2500 - 2570 / 2620 - 2690
8	880 - 915 / 925 - 960
9	1750 - 1785 / 1845 - 1880
10	1710 - 1770 / 2110 - 2170
11	1428 - 1453 / 1476 - 1501
12	698 - 716 / 728 - 746
13	746 - 758 / 776 - 788
14	758 - 768 / 788 - 798
17	704 - 716 / 734 - 746

TDD

Banda	Frequências UL/DL (MHz)
33, 34	1900 - 1920 / 2010 - 2025
35, 36	1850 - 1910 / 1930 - 1990
37	1910 - 1930
38	2570 - 2620
39	1880 - 1920
40	2300 - 2400

Figura 6:   Frequencies Operated by the LTE Network

Source: (SIQUEIRA, 2011)

In FDD, downlink and uplink traffic are transmitted simultaneously in

separate frequencies. In TDD, downlink and uplink transmissions are discontinued on the same frequency. Generally speaking, FDD is more efficient and represents higher device and infrastructure volumes.

In theory, according to (3GPP, 2008), an LTE network can reach 300 Mbps in the downlink and 75 Mbps in the uplink with cell coverage in the 5 to 100 km range with slight degradation after 30 km. In real conditions, these values are 100 Mbps and 50 Mbps downlink and uplink respectively for the 20 MHz spectrum. This decrease is due to overheads and the limitations of the network infrastructure, which is the main cause of latency. The LTE network can maintain speed and latency when used in a device with a speed of up to 350 kilometres per hour, which can rise to 500 kilometres per hour depending on the network's operating frequency.

2.8 The *Handover*

In his article *"Handover Management in GSM cellular system"*, (KHAN, 2010) defines handover as the procedure of transferring a continuous call from one cell[2] to another cell as the user moves away from the coverage area of the cellular system, i.e. within an LTE network, handover occurs when the user moves their mobile device away from the tower they are connected to and approaches another tower. This happens mainly because the user experiences a poor connection and consequently has high packet loss rates as they move away from the coverage area, and in an attempt to solve this problem, the user's connection is automatically transferred to another cell with a more stable connection.

For handover to happen, the scenario basically has to consist of two or more towers and a device connected to a tower. For a better understanding, Figure 7 shows a basic scenario of an LTE network with a device on the verge of handover.

Considering user mobility, handover can occur in two ways: horizontally or vertically. According to (RICARDO, 2009) "Horizontal handover, in cellular networks, consists of transferring responsibility for data communication from one base station to another", i.e. establishing communication in a new tower and updating the network so that the device keeps its connections running.

On the other hand, when the cell change procedure takes place between different technologies, for example, between WLAN (Wireless Local Area Network) and WMAN (Wireless Metropolitan Area Network), the procedure is called vertical handover (SALES, 2009; DHIMAN; SANDHA, 2013). A vertical handover can present the same challenges as a horizontal handover, since it deals with the transition between forms of communication.

---

[2] Cell, in the context of the chapter, should be understood as the tower where the mobile device connects.

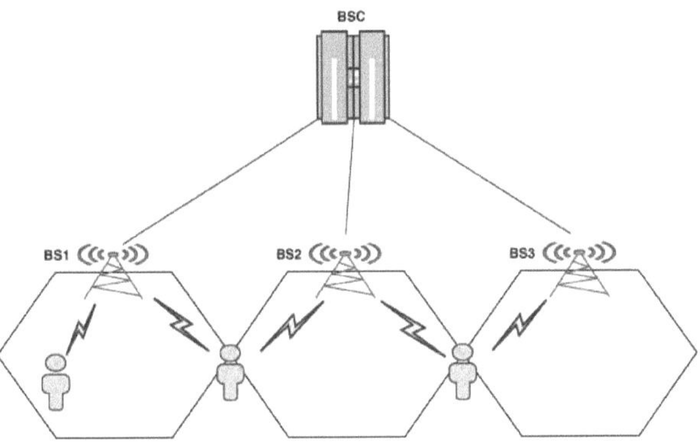

Figura 7:   Typical Horizontal *Handover* Scenario

Adapted from: (KADAH; NOLL, 2012)

access to the network. Figure 8 outlines a basic scenario where vertical handover can occur.

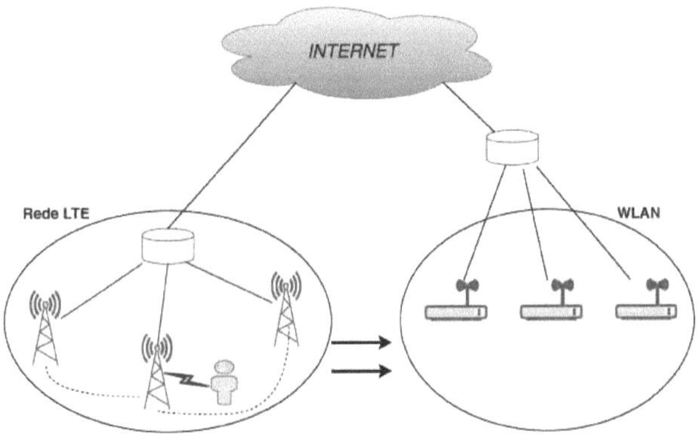

Figura 8:   Typical Scenario for Vertical *Handover*

Source: The Author

2.9   Impacts of *Handover*

Handover is considered a "costly procedure because it involves several tasks that can cause interruptions in the supply of services and degradation in application performance" (RICARDO, 2009). This becomes more serious as the frequency of migration and transition increases, since the number of handover incidents becomes greater. The most obvious challenge for the handover process is ensuring

the transition from one connection point to another is transparent both for the user and for upper layer protocols and applications.

As already mentioned, when the user connected to a tower is on the move, this mobility can trigger the handover process. Below are the main points where the damage from handover is greatest in an LTE network:

- Packet loss: Packet loss is common in any network during data transmissions, but at the exact moment of handover, packet loss in the LTE network skyrockets.

- Throughput: When the process of transferring from one cell to another takes place, the transmission rate drops considerably.

- Connection break: This is the most obvious and worrying impact on the handover process, as it can be visible and clear to the user.

It is important to emphasise that the handover process is not a problem in itself; on the contrary, it is the best alternative for maintaining the continuity of the service in use by the user when they face a poor connection due to the limited coverage of the cell to which they are connected. The efforts of the scientific community are focussed on finding solutions to mitigate the impact of handover.

An LTE network, together with the Internet, can be considered a distributed system, and according to (TANENBAW; DAVID, 2011) a distributed system must be transparent to the user. However, guaranteeing transparency in user mobility is not a trivial task, because in addition to the complexity of handover, it also involves the characteristics of a wireless network: size of cells, whether or not there is an intersection between them, etc.

2.10 Results

In this subsection, the results collected with the simulator will be shown graphically, in order to highlight the impacts on an LTE network during the handover procedure, and to support the study of the technology's performance evaluation.

Specifically, data on throughput, packet delay and jitter will be analysed as metrics for evaluating QoS (Quality of Service) in the network. An explanation will be given of the behaviour of each graph of these metrics in different LTE network simulation scenarios.

In order to achieve the research objectives, discrete event simulations were carried out. Simulation is a technique for evaluating the performance of a system based on the development of models, i.e. abstractions of reality that capture essential aspects of the object under study.

The scenarios schematised in the simulator were implemented using the tool's LTE library, which, among various functions, provides the LteHelper tool that allows all the nodes in the scenario (UEs and eNBs) to be structured with the particular technologies belonging to the LTE network. It is also worth mentioning the use of the MobilityModel module to grant and manage node mobility. The metrics used to analyse the results of the simulations were collected using the FlowMo- nitor class belonging to the simulator itself.

As the simulator is free software under the GNU GPLv2 licence, a large number of developers and researchers contribute to the software, allowing more modules to be created, some limitations to be overcome and the tool to be improved.

2.10.1   First Scenario

Figure 9 shows the scenario diagrammed in the simulator for carrying out the first simulation and analyses.

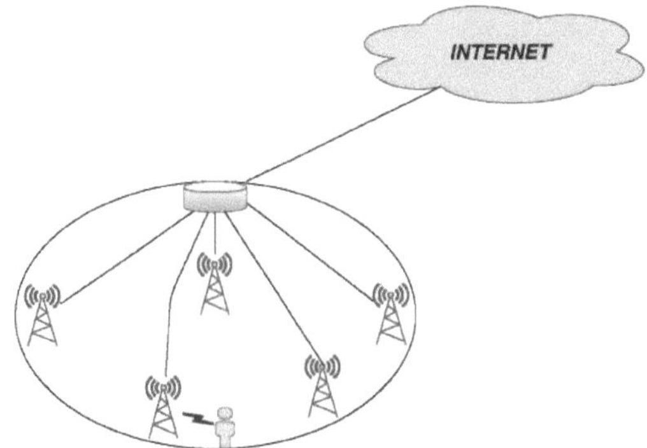

Figura 9:   First Simulation Scenario

Source: The Author

In the first simulation, a scenario with five towers and a node connected to one of the towers was schematised. The first simulation was carried out to analyse the impact of handover on the LTE network, mainly on data rates, i.e. throughput, packet delay and jitter. Table 1 shows the parameters used in the first simulation.

The results obtained in the first simulation show the behaviour of throughput, delay and jitter, especially during the handover procedure. Figure 10 shows the performance of the network through the behaviour of the throughput.

Figure 10 shows the flow behaviour. It can be seen that while the node remains connected to the first tower, the data transmission received increases dramatically, reaching 1.63 Mbps as a result of the application running on the UE,

Table 1: Parameters for the First Simulation

Parameters	Values
Number of users	A connected node
Simulation Time	150 seconds
Technology	LTE network
Internet traffic	100 Gigabit/s
Application Traffic	1 Gigabit/s
Application package size	100000 bit
Node speed	20 metres/s

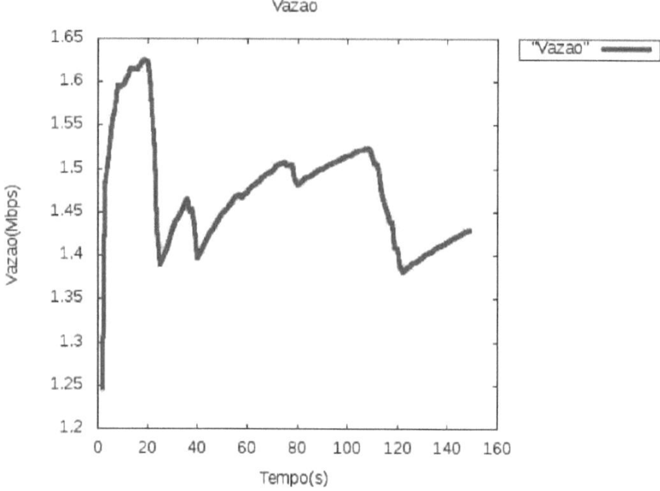

Figura 10: Flow - First Scenario

Source: The Author

a factor responsible for the self-peak observed in the flow rate. However, at 20 seconds into the simulation, the flow rate fell sharply due to the handover procedure that was triggered at this point, affecting the data transmission rate required by the UE application. Due to the node's mobility, at one point the tower's coverage was unable to provide a good service, so it was necessary to transfer the node's connection to another tower.

At 23 seconds into the simulation, the data transmission rate increases again, which is caused by the node connecting, after the handover, to a tower with a better quality of service. This explains the growth in the flow curve between 23 seconds and 35 seconds of simulation. However, at 36 seconds into the simulation, the handover procedure is triggered again, due to the node facing a low quality of service offered by the tower to which it is connected, explaining the drop in the flow curve at 36 seconds into the simulation.

At 40 seconds into the simulation, the node's connection is established in a new tower with a better quality of service to offer. As a result, the data transmission rate increases again, as can be seen in the behaviour of the flow curve after 40 seconds of simulation.

It is important to note that at 110 seconds into the simulation, the handover procedure is triggered again, causing a decrease in the data transmission rate. As the node moves further away from the tower, it is unable to provide a quality signal, so the node's connection is transferred to another tower with a better quality of service. At the moment of the handover, the flow curve drops. However, at 120 seconds into the simulation, the node's connection is established on a tower with better signal quality, which allows data transmission to grow, as evidenced by the growth in the flow curve after 120 seconds of simulation. Figure 11 shows the behaviour of the packet delay during the simulation.

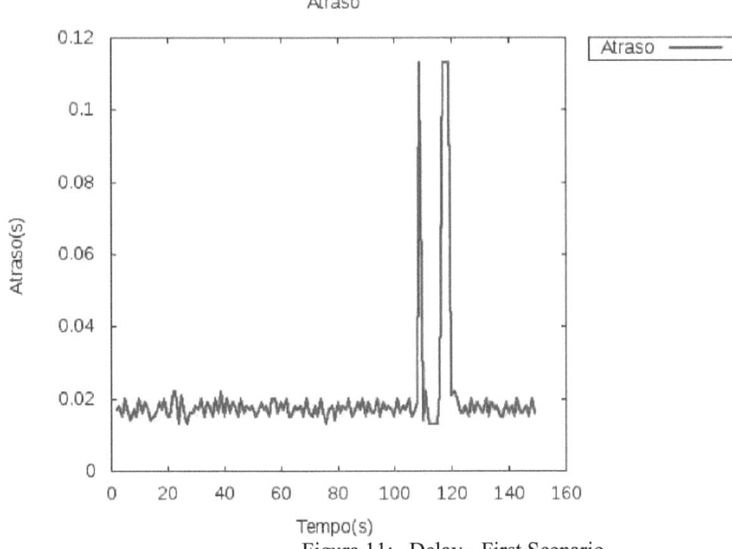

Figura 11: Delay - First Scenario

Source: The Author

Figure 11 shows the variation in delay during the simulation. It can be seen that at 110 seconds into the simulation, the moment when the handover occurred and one of the moments when the flow curve drops, the packet delay reached a high peak, reaching 0.1 Is. Before the handover is triggered again, the packet delay, between 40 seconds and 100 seconds of simulation, behaves in a stable manner, i.e. without sudden variations. The stability in the standard variation of the packet delay is disturbed when the node, between 100 seconds and 120 seconds of simulation, is about to perform the handover.

High packet delay rates slow down the node connection and are the main cause of network overheads.

It's important to note that after 120 seconds of simulation, after the handover occurred, the variation in packet delay stabilised. This was due to the node establishing a connection to the tower that offered it the best quality of service. This process can be seen in the stable behaviour of the delay graph (Figure 11) after 120 seconds.

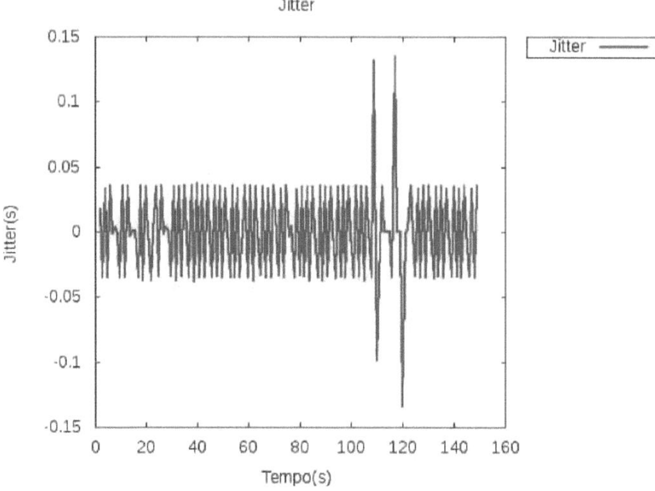

Figura 12:   Jitter - First Scenario

Source: The Author

Jitter can be defined as the statistical variation in packet delay in a network. For this reason, during the handover procedure, at 110 seconds into the simulation, jitter, like delay, also peaked, but then normalised after the process, as shown in Figure 12.

During the handover, between 110 seconds and 120 seconds of simulation, jitter reaches a peak of 0.14 seconds, a high value compared to the jitter values before the handover. It is important to emphasise that a very high delay variation produces irregular packet reception, generating a greater number of packet losses in the network. After 120 seconds of simulation, the jitter variation rates stabilised, due to the node being connected to a tower with a better coverage area.

2.10.1.1 Second   Scenario

Figure 13 shows the schematised scenario for the second simulation. It is important to note that there is now more than one node connected to the network.

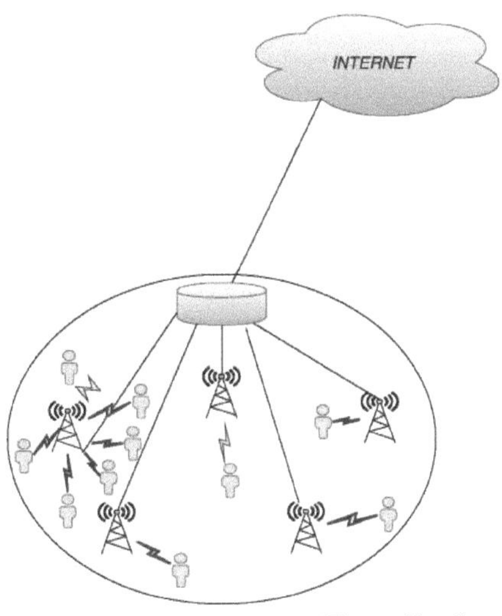

Figura 13:   Second Simulation Scenario

Source: The Author

The second simulation added ten more connected nodes, which had a greater impact on the network compared to the first simulation scenario, as all ten nodes were running the same application and using the same bandwidth for data traffic. Table 2 shows the parameters used in this phase.

Table 2: Parameters for the Second Simulation

Parameters	Values
Number of users	Ten connected nodes
Simulation Time	200 Seconds
Technology	LTE network
Internet traffic	100 Gigabit/s
Application Traffic	1 Gigabit/s
Application package size	100000 bit
Node speed	20 metres/s

With the addition of nine more nodes to the scenario, the network's performance will undergo a noticeable change. Figure 14 shows the flow behaviour after the nine nodes have been added.

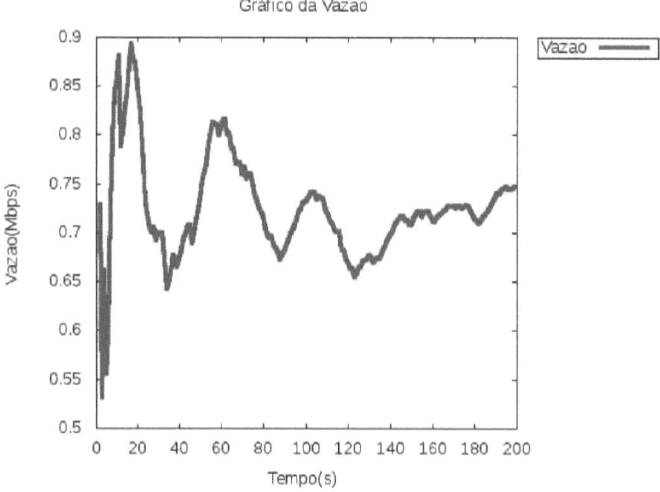

Figura 14:   Flow - Second Scenario

Source: The Author

Figure 14 shows the behaviour of the flow in the first node. It can be seen that after 20 seconds of simulation, the handover process is triggered and the flow rate drops. This can be seen by the decline in the flow curve shown in the graph after 20 seconds of simulation.

Flow stability is achieved again after 38 seconds of simulation, when the handover ends and the node connects to the tower that offers it the best coverage area. It's important to note that at this point there are nine nodes running the same application. For this reason, in addition to the handover, the graph shows fluctuations in flow.

It is important to note that as the node moves away from the tower to which it is connected, after 20 seconds of simulation, the data transmission rate required by the application running on the node decreases. This is due to the drop in signal quality received by the node as it moves away from the coverage area. Figure 15 shows the oscillations in packet delay in the network.

With the addition of ten nodes to the network, the packet delay reached higher peaks during the handover, which is evident after 20 seconds of simulation, when the delay reaches 1 second (Figure 15), i.e. a longer time compared to the delay graph of the previous scenario. Furthermore, at the end of the simulation, after 140 seconds, the delay rate does not reach 0.02 seconds, as seen in Graph 2 over the same period.

It's interesting to note that after 40 seconds of simulation up to 100 seconds of simulation, the delay variation is reduced, due to the fact that the node connection is

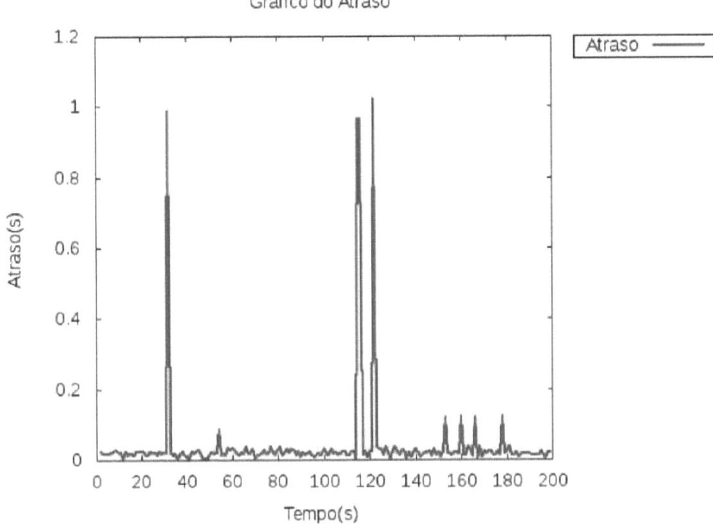

Figura 15:   Delay - Second Scenario

Source: The Author

established on the target tower and therefore receive better signal quality. Jitter will also behave differently in this scenario, as shown in Figure 16.

In Figure 16, jitter does not reach the lowest values as it did in the previous scenario. After 20 seconds of simulation, the handover is triggered, at which point the jitter oscillation time is longer than it was 19 seconds earlier. After the handover, the oscillation time still reaches a higher peak, but after 125 seconds of simulation the jitter reaches stability with a shorter time. This is evident in the graph in Figure 16 after 125 seconds of simulation.

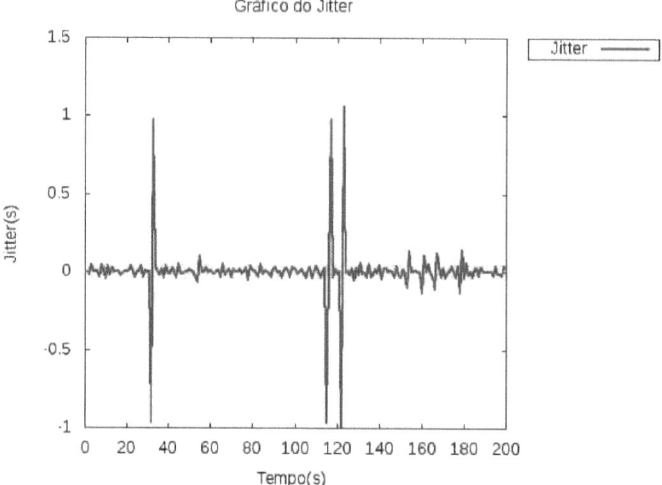

Figura 16:   Jitter - Second Scenario

Source: The Author

CHAPTER 3

Mesh networks

Author: Rodrigo da Silva Saraiva[3]

3.1   Overview

Wireless local area networks can be organised as infrastructure, Ad-Hoc or Mesh networks. In infrastructure networks, a base station called an access point (AP) manages a certain group of devices, intermediating their transmissions. For devices to be able to communicate over the wireless network, they must first associate with an AP. In adhoc networks there is no such central station, so any device on the network can communicate with anyone within range. In Mesh networks, which can be seen as a special case of Ad-Hoc networks, devices are able to determine their own transmission routes within the network. As a result, a node that wants to carry out a transmission can use other nodes as intermediaries to forward frames to destinations outside its range.

In Mesh networks, stations communicate directly, without the need for an access point. If the destination station is outside the signal range of the node wishing to transmit, the frames to that station can be forwarded by intermediate stations. In this way, the stations have the function of routers, enabling them to forward packets in order to maintain connectivity to all the devices on the network. To do this, stations need to be strategically allocated in the scenario to cover the largest possible area, acting as a static infrastructure to provide connectivity to user devices. In the case of stations that are only one hop away, this makes it possible to
obtain better utilisation of the wireless channel by reducing the number of transmissions required. Mesh networks have the ability to self-organise, so that new paths between stations can be formed if there is a change in the network topology (e.g. a new station is dropped or added, a link is broken, a route is overloaded).

The structure of the Mesh network within the scope of IEEE 802.11 wireless networks is the subject of the IEEE 802.lis standard, which was drawn up in 2004 by the Task Group "s" (TGs). The final proposal was approved in July 2011 and published at the end of November 2011, forming part of the IEEE 802.11 - 2012 standard.

The great advance of wireless networks has led to the emergence of mesh networks, which are highly usable, especially in areas with difficult access, as well as in areas where wired service providers cannot reach. In this network architecture, a node is seen as a mobile router, increasing the radius of the network so that the organisation of each node can insert and communicate with other

---

[3]Bachelor in Information Systems, UfPA, Faculty of Computing, Email: andiiforce@gmail.com

nodes, using a multi hop routing protocol for transmission.

According to this standard, stations can communicate directly and connectivity throughout the network must be provided through path discovery carried out directly at the link layer. The 802.lis standard makes use of dynamic path discovery protocols, so that in the event of a change in the current network structure, such as a station being dropped or added, the network adapts automatically, without breaking connectivity. The emergence of wireless mesh networks has made it possible to popularise the Internet, creating so-called "digital cities", where access is provided through access points strategically distributed on university campuses, commercial buildings, hospitals, etc. The advantages of this technology benefit various segments of society, creating a communication network that is easy to deploy and low cost, and can be expanded easily.

The evolutionary process of telecommunications technologies together with information technology, together with the growing need to keep people connected to the Internet, has increasingly led to the development of wireless networks. The growth of wireless networks in conjunction with information technology is aimed at meeting needs such as: mobile phone services, wireless networks, satellite data transmissions, radio providers, as well as the main proposal of this work, the free distribution of the Internet. Like wired networks, wireless networks can be of two types: LAN and WAN. WAN or WWAN (Wireless Wide Area Network) type wireless networks are mainly based on mobile phone networks, which were initially used for voice communication, but nowadays it is quite possible to transfer data over this medium.

3.2   The IEEE 802.11 Standard

The IEEE 802.11 standard defines the standardisation of the physical (PHY) and media access control (MAC) layers for wireless networks. A network based on this standard is made up of the following components:

- BSS (Basic Service Set) - Corresponds to a wireless communication network;

- STA (Stations) - Workstations that communicate within the BSS;

- AP (Access Point) - Node responsible for coordinating communication between the STAs within the BSS;

- ESS (Extended Service Set) - These are nearby BSS cells that intersect and the APs are connected to the same network. As a result, an STA can move from one BSS to another while maintaining its connection to the network.

Networks characterised by the 802.11 standard can operate in two different modes: Infrastructure mode and Ad-hoc mode.

3.2.1   Infrastructure networks

It has two types of elements: Mobile Stations (MS) and Access Points (AP). The access points are responsible for connecting the mobile stations to the fixed network. Each point has control of a certain coverage area (BSA - Basic Set Area). Data transfer in these networks always takes place between a station and an access point (AP). APs are special nodes responsible for capturing and relaying messages sent by stations. Data transfer never takes place directly between two stations. The AP can also act as a bridge to another network (wired or wireless). Networks with infrastructure lose some of the flexibility that wireless networks can offer, for example, they become unusable in the event of an earthquake that destroys the entire network infrastructure or just its APs.

3.2.2   Ad-Hoc Networks

Ad hoc networks will be used as the basis for the scenarios simulated in our work, so we will focus more on their technologies and advantages, as well as their support for the protocols that will be used in the simulations. Ad Hoc networks are characterised by not having any infrastructure to support communication. The various mobile devices are located in a coverage area of the other nodes and establish point-to-point communication between them. No AP is needed to control access to the medium. A station A can only communicate with B if B is

within A's radius of action or if there are one or more stations between A and B that can forward the message, depending on the routing protocol. By radius of action we mean the coverage area of a station, i.e. all the geographical points where the signal from this station reaches with a minimum of clarity. (AKYILDIZ; WANG; WANG, 2005) In an Ad Hoc network, the complexity and processing rate of each station is high because every station must be equipped with mechanisms for accessing the medium, as well as for communicating with other stations, mechanisms for controlling problems with congested paths or broken links, as well as mechanisms for providing a certain quality of service. When nodes move, the resulting change in the network topology must be informed to all the other nodes, so that topology information can be updated frequently. These networks are tolerant of faults and the removal of stations (nodes), because their organisation and control do not depend on just a few specific nodes; all nodes have the task of routing and relaying packets. Similarly, new nodes can easily be added to these networks. Network core functions generally use the familiar traditional routing protocols, which implement routing techniques called distance-vector or hop-by-hop or link-state, used in the operation of wired networks. In contrast to this type of solution, the goal of mobile wireless ad hoc networks is to extend the concept of mobility to allow fully autonomous mobile wireless domains made up of a set of nodes (which can be routers or stations) to themselves form an ad-hoc mesh network routing infrastructure.

3.3 The 802.lis Standard - Wireless Mesh Networks

According to (AKYILDIZ; WANG; WANG, 2005), Mesh networks were funded in the 1990s by the US military at the Defence Advanced Research Projects Agency (DARPA), with the aim of end-to-end communication without the need for a central station. It was used by the military during the Iraq war for communication between different teams, where each element - soldiers, tanks and helicopters - was a station on the network. For the military, this would avoid the fragility of an attack on a central station, if one existed. Within the scope of the IEEE 802.11 standard, a Mesh wireless local area network was defined as follows: A Mesh BSS (MBSS - Mesh Basic Service Set) is an IEEE 802.11 WLAN made up of autonomous nodes. Within the MBSS, all nodes establish wireless links with neighbouring nodes to exchange messages. In addition, using this network's ability to communicate using multiple hops, there can be communication between nodes that have no direct link between them. From a data delivery point of view, the network functions as a single broadcast domain. Thus, all nodes in an MBSS communicate directly at link level, even if they are not within direct range. The multiple hop capability has the effect of increasing the range of the nodes, and thus extending the connectivity of the wireless local area network. 17Mesh networks, like Ad Hoc networks, are characterised by the fact that they do not require

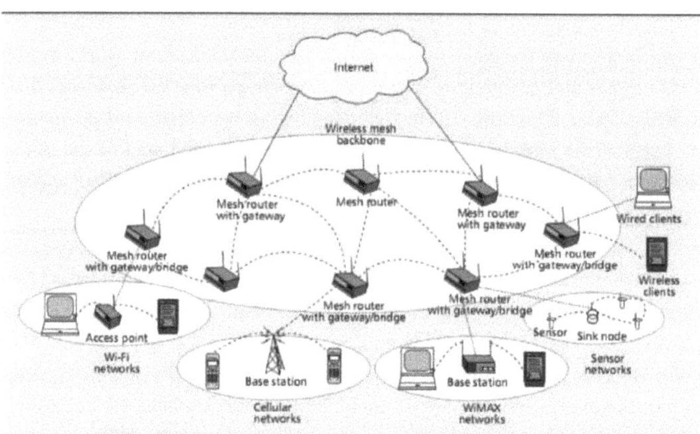

Figura 17: Representation of the Scenario with a Mesh Network, the Organisation and Communication of the Nodes.

Source: (AKYILDIZ; WANG; WANG, 2005)

an access point for communication between the devices, as they can communicate directly. Each device acts as a router within the wireless network, forwarding information from its neighbours in a cooperative manner, i.e. communication between devices via one or more hops. Mesh networks are a variation of the Ad Hoc network genre, but they differ in that Ad Hoc networks are networks with a highly dynamic, non-infrastructured topology, and their stations can be mobile. Because of this, they need routing protocols that allow this to happen with the minimum of problems, unlike Mesh networks which have a backbone made up of wireless routers that keep the network with more stable routes, having a relatively static hierarchy, and may have one or more access points with the external network. Another point is the routing protocol, because while in the Ad Hoc network the users must agree to use the same protocol, in the Mesh network this is part of the technology itself and is therefore transparent to the user. In Ad Hoc networks, routing takes place at the network layer, but in Mesh networks it takes place at the link layer. Mesh networks are also characterised by the ability of their devices to organise themselves in the event of a topology change. If a station is lost, the network reorganises itself, forming new routes. Due to its capacity for self-organisation, the network automatically incorporates a new Mesh station. Self-organisation in the Mesh network helps choose the best paths between devices, so that messages are transmitted to a neighbouring station that is best suited to reaching the destination. As a result, these networks present challenges such as the development of routing protocols capable of dealing with changes in the network topology and also choosing routes that provide transmissions with fewer errors and better utilisation of the channel.

In a Mesh network, new stations are incorporated automatically due to the use of dynamic routing protocols in the link layer. This happens without the need for user interference, offering users convenience and ease of access. This feature of this type of network can be useful for various applications. These include home, institutional and metropolitan networks.

17.3.1   Elements and Architecture of Mesh Networks in the 802.11 standard

The Mesh network is made up of autonomous and interdependent stations that act as routers, which can communicate directly or via multiple hops, forwarding frames to their destination or using neighbouring stations to reach it. In addition, they can provide access to other stations not participating in the Mesh network, and even access to the Internet. To this end, the IEEE 802.11 standard has defined the following elements for the Mesh network:

- Client or Station (STA) - This is a station that requests services, but does not pass on data, nor does it participate in the path discovery carried out by the routing protocols;

- Mesh Point (MP) - A station that participates in the formation and operation of the Mesh network, passing on data and participating in route discovery;

- Mesh Access Point (MAP) - This is a MAP attached to a node that is providing Internet access to clients (STA) in a given area;

- Mesh Portal Point (MPP) - This is an MP with the special functionality of acting as a gateway between the Mesh network and the external network (Internet, for example);

- MBSS (Mesh Basic Service Set) - A group of stations that make up the Mesh network. It can contain MP, MAP and MPP. An MBSS can contain more than one MPP.

Mesh network stations create links with their neighbours and communicate via paths that are discovered dynamically, using the HWMP (Hybrid Wireless Mesh Protocol) routing protocol by default. Transmissions in this type of network are the result of the existence of interconnected nodes that must communicate and send data from one side of the network to the other, but overcome failures caused by nodes that may simply stop working at a given time. What's more, these networks must be able to create and/or decide the best routes on their own and dynamically, adapting to the functioning or otherwise of the nodes around them. When an event like this happens, the network must find another way for the information to reach its destination, looking for other available nodes that can, without passing through the damaged point, take the information to the destination outlined in the route. The fact that mesh networks can tolerate such failures makes them sufficiently reliable.

3.4 Routing Protocols

IEEE 802.lis proposes the HWMP (Hybrid Mesh Wireless Protocol) protocol as the basis for using routing for mesh networks. The HWMP protocol is based on the AODV (Ad Hoc On-

Demand Distance Vector) protocol, adapted for the link layer. The HWMP protocol provides two modes of operation: On-Demand Routing and Proactive Routing (CONNER et ah, 2006).

On-Demand Mode: Route discovery in this mode is only carried out when necessary. For example, if a station needs to transmit a frame to a destination but doesn't know a suitable route to that destination, on-demand path discovery is initiated. This mode allows MPs to communicate using end-to-end paths, as well as not congesting the network, since communication for route discovery is only initiated when transmission is required. In on-demand mode, path discovery begins when a mesh station has data to transmit to an unknown destination. It transmits a Path Request (PREQ) informing the other nodes of the destination. Each station that receives this PREQ creates a route to the source, with metric updates and routing messages. If the station has valid routing information for the destination or the station is the destination itself, a Path Reply frame (PREP) is generated. Figure 18.

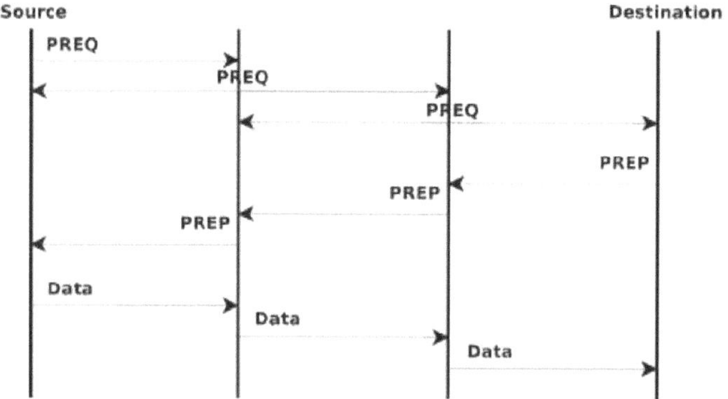

Figura 18:   Representation of the On-Demand Mode route discovery scheme

Source: Author

Proactive Mode: In this mode, the functionality of proactively building a path tree is added to the on-demand mode. This tree is based on an MP, in which the active PREQ (Path Request) or RANN (Root Announcement) mechanisms are used to discover paths to all the other stations on the network. The active PREQ mechanism

creates the paths from each MP to the transmitting source station, and can be bidirectional. The RANN mechanism creates bidirectional paths between the source station and each MP in the network. HWMP has the flexibility of on-demand route discovery and efficient proactive routing for its Mesh portals. According to (AKYILDIZ; WANG; WANG, 2005), during the path discovery process, each station will contribute its metric calculations by adding or updating data in the management frames dedicated to exchanging routing information. Regardless of the mode of operation (proactive or reactive), HWMP functions are implemented by the following management agents:

Path Request (PREQ) - These frames are sent in broadcast by a PM who wants to find a path to another PM.

Path Reply (PREP) - These frames are sent by the destination MP in response to receiving a path request (PREQ).

Path Error (PERR) - These frames are used to notify that a path is no longer available. Announcement (RANN) - Announcement of the originating station - these frames are used by the station announcing itself as the originating station for that transmission. As seen above, there are two ways in which HWMP behaves, and the RANN frame is used in one of them. Figure 19.

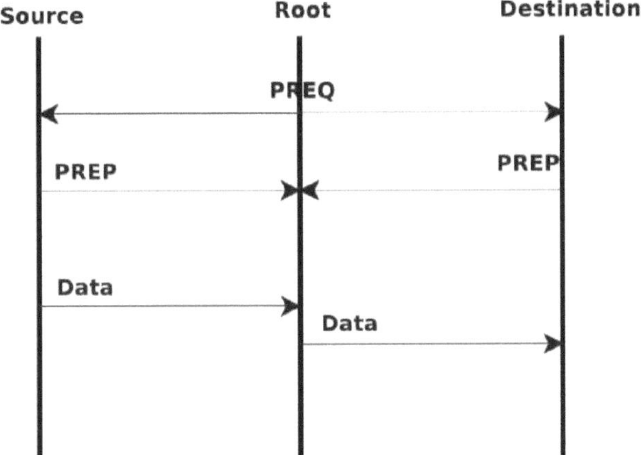

Figura 19:   Representation of the Pro-Active Mode route discovery scheme.

Source: Author

3.5 Mesh Network Simulations

A total of up to 35 nodes were used in the simulations, randomly allocated throughout the scenario and transmitting information to each other. Each node communicates with the other 34 using the mesh network's own routing protocol (HWMP), as well as two other routing protocols recognised by the simulator (AODV and OLSR), in order to compare the results and analyse the difference in performance between the protocols.

In addition to the simulator itself, we also used tools to analyse the traffic of the nodes that were created in the source code, as well as tools to plot the graphs generated using the information collected in the simulation. We used NetAnim (Network Animator), a network animator that graphically illustrates how the nodes were arranged in the scenario, as well as how transmissions were made and the direction of each one. It was extremely important in this work. Another piece of software used was Gnuplot, a graph projection tool, which was used to compare the performance of the other topologies, protocols, number of nodes in each scenario and simulation time. We also used the Urban Mobility Simulator (SUMO) to create the routes in the city of Castanhal where the nodes would be allocated and to have a real assessment of the performance of this traffic between the nodes. Figure 20.

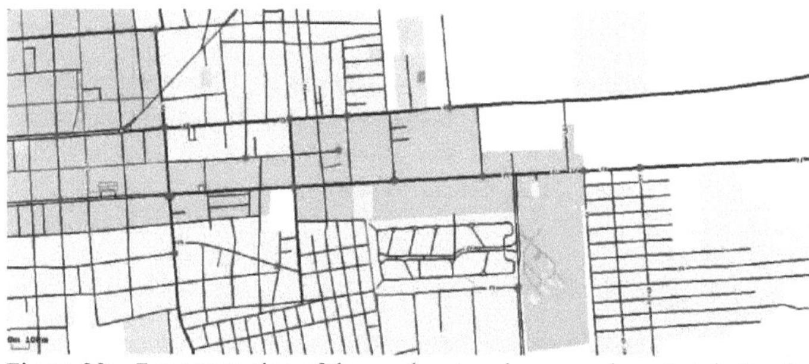

Figura 20:   Representation of the mesh network on an urban stretch, the distribution of nodes across the simulated scenario, implemented in the simulator, generated by SUMO

Source: Author

The progress made with studies on mesh networks has led to numerous simulations being carried out in different scenarios of possible regions and organisations of the nodes, as well as changes in the transmission rate and size of the packets used. In this final stage of the simulation, the code used was the standard Mesh network code (mesh.cc) found in the simulator itself. The other tools were implemented manually in this code, as were the libraries and other parameters used. A code that also provided support in this work and can also be found in the simulator's directories was "hwmp.cc", which is responsible for managing the mesh network's own routing protocol, and it was necessary to change it to implement other protocols, as shown in the figure below.

Node ID	Node IP	Protocol Node Routing	Transmitted Packet Size	Total From We
00	10.0.0.1	HWMP	1024 bytes	35
01	10.0.0.2	HWMP	1024 bytes	
02	10.0.0.3	HWMP	1024 bytes	
03	10.0.0.4	HWMP	1024 bytes	
04	10.0.0.5	HWMP	1024 bytes	
05	10.0.0.35	HWMP	1024 bytes	

Simulation Time	Technology used	Type of Application
100 seconds	Wireless nodes Wireless Link Mesh topology	UDP

Figura 21:   Illustration of the data on the nodes used to build the simulation, as well as their parameters.

Source: Author

3.6 Performance Evaluation of Network Protocols

The simulations implemented a wireless mesh local area network in an urban setting. Using the Mesh network technology with the IEEE 802.1is protocol provided in the simulator. The aim of the simulation was to enable communication between the nodes as well as to define the best route to be chosen by the nodes for transmissions. Using the scenarios, experiments were carried out to observe the self-organisation of the nodes, the flow rate and the delays in the delivery and loss of frames, as well as evaluating the performance of the network with the protocols used.

3.6.1   Results

It is possible to analyse the duration of the simulation, a parameter that can be defined in the simulation algorithm. Other data can also be obtained by building the code, such as the flow rate in Mbps, the IP address of the packets involved in the simulation and the monitor's identification. The six nodes in Figure 21 were inserted into a scenario where their positions were configured manually using coordinates. The protocol used was the standard for mesh networks, HWMP (Hybrid Wireless Mesh Protocol). The simulation lasted around 100 seconds. The main objective was to measure the flow of the nodes in order to have a basis for subsequent simulations. The packets have a default size of 1024 bytes, but their size was purposely halved in order to obtain a variation in traffic performance. Figure 22.

As previously discussed, mesh networks are similar to other forms of wireless communication, but their difference lies in the organisation of the nodes, where

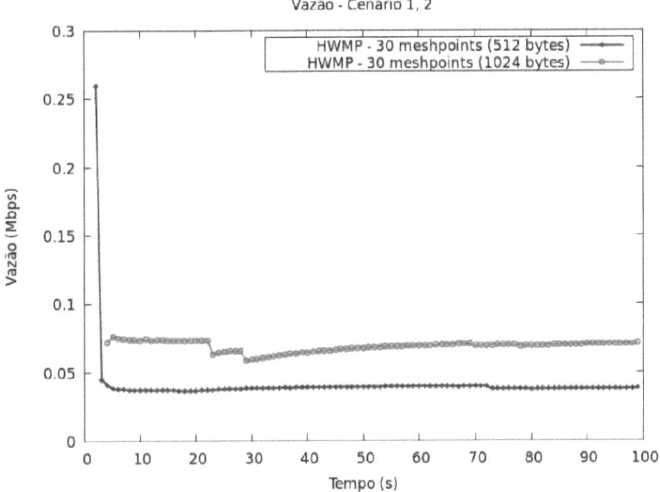

Figura 22:   Performance comparison between scenarios transmitting packets of different sizes

Source: Author

Each node can be a router, so a fact that directly affects network performance, in addition to the location of each node in the scenario, is also the size of the packets that are transmitted on the network. The same parameters used in the simulation illustrated in Figure 22 were repeated and simulated again, but with the size of the packets normalised to 1024 Kbytes each, in order to see a change in performance and make a comparison. Another metric that also directly influences network performance, in addition to packet size, is the number of nodes being distributed in the scenario. Depending on the routing protocol and the distance of these nodes from each other, network performance can drop or increase. See Figure 23, where we use the same protocol as the mesh network (HWMP), but vary the number of nodes to see the difference in data flow in the scenario.

Note that when the scenario reaches a certain number of devices communicating, performance starts to behave differently, because numerous factors also interfere with transmission efficiency. Here we also explain another factor that also greatly interferes with the performance of a network, but this one is more specific, because it is about network options that can be chosen by the network administrator. These are routing protocols, the efficiency of which varies from situation to situation. Figure 24.

As the simulation progresses, you can see that the performance of a scenario starts to behave differently, because factors such as the number of nodes also affect transmission efficiency. Figure 25 shows

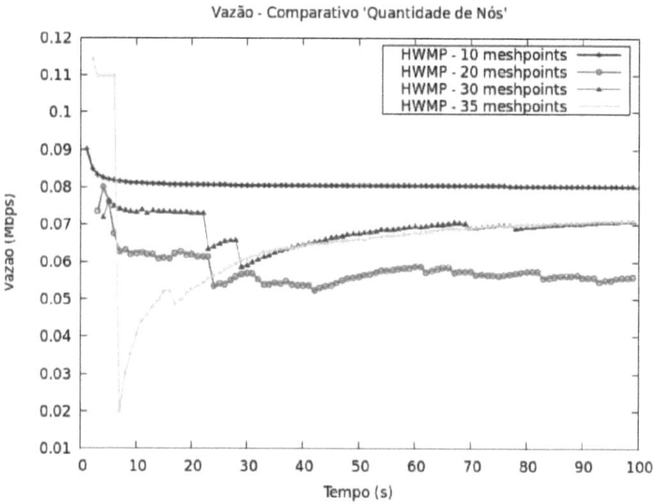

Figura 23:   Flow rate of the mesh.cc algorithm, comparing networks with 10, 20, 30 and 35 active nodes

Source: Author

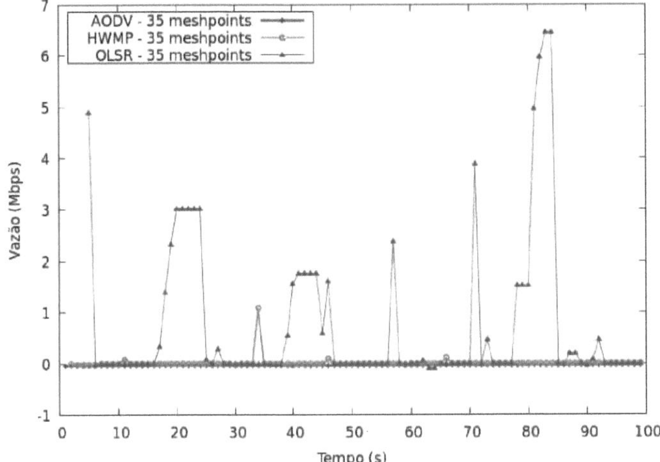

Figura 24:   Delay rate of the mesh.cc algorithm, comparing networks with the same number of nodes (35), but with different routing protocols

Source: Author

There is also another factor that directly interferes with network performance. These are routing protocols, whose efficiency varies from situation to situation. Whether the protocol handles packet retransmission, whether it is proactive in discovering its neighbours' routes or whether it has a fault tolerance mechanism in place, all have a direct influence on network performance. The fact that the HWMP protocol has all the advantages of the other two protocols compared to it explains its better performance in the graph.

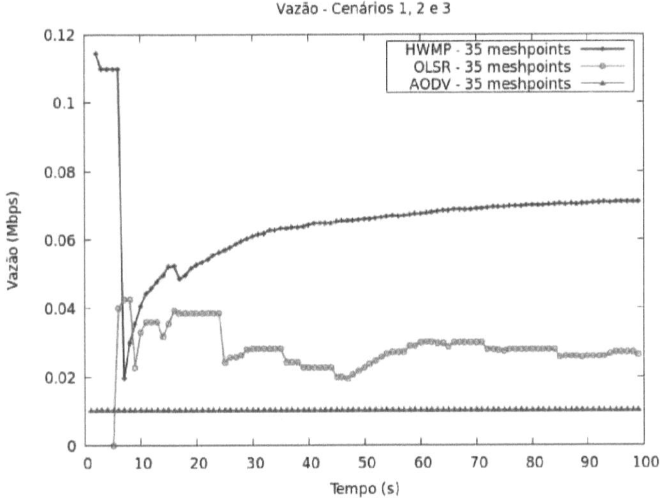

Figura 25: Throughput of the mesh.cc algorithm, comparing networks with the same number of nodes (30), but with different routing protocols

Source: Author

An analysis of the graphs shows the difference in transmission behaviour. This is because although the number of nodes is the same between the scenarios, the protocols behave differently and have different decision-making criteria. The idea of "best path" changes from protocol to protocol, an example of which is that in AODV, the best path will always be the one with the node that makes the most requests, since it works on demand. In OLSR, on the other hand, the path that has the link available at the time of the request will be chosen, regardless of the number of hops it has to make until it reaches its destination, making its choice not always the most appropriate. As HWMP combines the best of the two protocols and tries to make up for their deficiencies, this explains why it has the most acceptable performance in Figure 6. Bearing in mind that these long-range, cost-effective networks are considerably recent, studies on them are increasingly valued, and it is common to look for help in forums to ask questions about the technologies.

of work is constant. After analysing the simulations, it was observed that graphically the algorithms behave similarly, despite the change in maximum packet size, but if we look at the numbers/metrics that are generated by xgraph, we see that the difference in behaviour between them is significant, both in simulation time and in performance.

34

CHAPTER 4

Vehicle networks

Author: Hygor Jardim da Silva[4]

4.1 Overview

Mobile wireless networks currently represent a widespread paradigm of computer network and wireless telecommunications technologies and computing at the same time as interactive computing and ubiquitous computing are becoming a reality. With the evolution of these concepts, the emergence of new ideas stemming from them and the growth in the current needs of computer networks, an important mode of network operation has emerged based on Mobile *Ad-hoc Networks* (MANETs) known as VANET (Vehicular *Ad-hoc Networks*) (LI; WANG; CAROLINA, 2007).

VANETs are mobile networks made up mainly of vehicles travelling on a road network and also of fixed bases on the network's infrastructure. VANETs are networks that are in the field of MANETs, so the challenges encountered in implementing MANETs are also challenges in implementing VANETs (REICHARDT et ah, 2002).

There are two types of communication in VANETs. The first, more similar to communication in a MANET, is communication between vehicles called V2V *(Vehicle to Vehicle)*. In this type of communication, the network topology is totally dynamic and the nodes behave in a self-organising and self-managing way, making it a challenge to develop routing protocols for this type of communication where the exchange of information is not possible.

routing messages becomes large. The second is a communication made up of fixed bases, the RSUs *(Road Side Units)* in the infrastructure of the road network called V2I *(Vehicle-to-Infrastructure)* (TALIWAL et ah, 2004).

Each vehicle in a vehicular mobile network functions as a node that receives and sends messages, or as a router that receives a packet and forwards it on to the recipient. Communication between vehicles is usually medium or short distance. Some nodes are stationary and are located at strategic points on the road, such as restaurants and petrol stations. Communication with these fixed bases usually has a longer range.

Packet routing is simple since each packet is delivered with just one hop, and the position of

---

[4]Undergraduate student in Computer Engineering, UFPA, Faculty of Computing, E-mail: hygorjardim@gmail.com

each base is known. When a vehicle sends a public message, it simply sends it to the bases and they broadcast it. You could also consider systems that back up data from vehicles parked at home, making the home a private base.

VANETs have been emerging in recent years along with new technologies to integrate the capabilities of wireless next generation networks (WNGN) for vehicles. This type of network configuration is an important mode of operation for today's mobile networks and has been developed with the idea of providing ubiquitous connectivity during vehicle mobility along roads, streets, avenues and even highways, connecting vehicles to the external[5] *backbone*, the Internet via various computer network and telecommunications technologies, homes or workplaces and efficient vehicle-to-vehicle communications that enable *Intelligent Transportation* Systems (ITS). In this way, VANETs are also known as inter-vehicle communications (IVC) or *vehicle-to-vehicle* communications (V2V) (PAIER et ah, 2007).

ITS is the main application of VANETs. ITS includes a variety of applications, such as co-operative traffic monitoring, traffic flow control, blind crossing, collision and accident prevention and detection, nearby information services and real-time diversions route computing. Another important application for VANETs is to provide Internet connectivity for vehicular devices (clients) while they are in motion, so that users can download music, send e-mails or for vehicle passengers to play games, as outlined in Figure 26.

This type of network can also exploit the user's context to facilitate access to different information among the above, such as commerce applications, other forms of entertainment, road traffic control, electronic toll collection, as well as checking other information about traffic conditions (alerts, flow, accidents, etc.), positively assisting users and keeping access roads cleaner, more accessible and less congested with intelligent traffic routing by

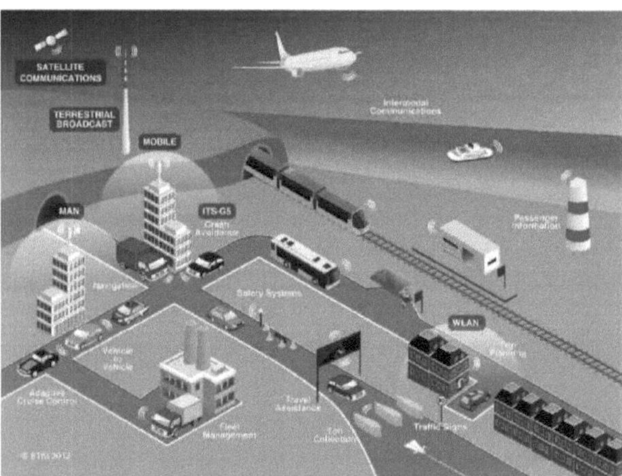

Figure 26: Intelligent Transport Systems.

---

[5]Backbone is the part of the computer network infrastructure that inter-connects different networks and provides a path for the exchange of data between these different networks.

large cities, corroborating the context of the smart cities of the Future Internet (FI*)*.

In addition, the advent of Interactive Digital TV and the growth in the use of mobile devices with internet access has contributed to the emergence of a new category of applications that make it possible to exploit the user's mobility and context in order to help them carry out their daily tasks. However, it is necessary to use technologies that are appropriate to the local reality and that offer greater quality, range, performance and security.

VANET or IVC has attracted significant attention from the scientific community, academia and especially industry from a very early stage. One of the first studies into IVC was initiated by Japan's JSK (Automotive Traffic and Driving Electronics Technology Association) in the early 80s. Later, California Path and Chauífeur also demonstrated the technique of coupling two or more vehicles together electronically to form a train.

At the beginning of this new millennium, the European *CarTALK 2000* project tried to investigate problems related to safe and comfortable driving based on communications between vehicles.

In recent years, there has been a rapid growth in mobile wireless technologies and an exponential increase in articles on VANETs or IVCs being published in leading journals by the various academies around the world, such as various workshops like the ACM *International Workshop on Vehicular ad-hoc Networks* and the *International Workshop on Intelligent Transportation* and the standardisation of *IEEE 802. llp* by the respected IEEE

(Institute of Electrical and Electronic Engineers) with the prediction of work plans formalised in mid-2009.

4.2 Network Architecture and Characteristics

The architecture of vehicular networks defines how the nodes are organised and communicate. There are currently three main architectures: pure ad-*hoc* (Vehicular ad-hoc NETwork - VANET), infrastructure or hybrid. In the *ad-hoc* architecture*,* vehicles communicate without any external support or centralising element. To do this, the vehicles act as routers and forward traffic via multiple hops.

Although this is the simplest configuration, as it does not require any type of infrastructure, its main disadvantage is the connectivity of the network, which depends on the density and mobility pattern of the vehicles. To avoid connectivity problems, the infrastructure architecture uses static nodes distributed along streets or roads. These static nodes act as access points for *IEEE 802.11* networks, also in infrastructure mode. They centralise all network traffic, serving as intermediary communications nodes (ALVES et ah, 2008).

The advantage of infrastructure mode is increased connectivity and the possibility of communicating with other networks, such as the Internet. However, network connectivity is only guaranteed through a large number of fixed elements, which can increase network costs. Hybrid architecture is an intermediate solution between *ad-hoc* and infrastructure.

In hybrid architecture, a minimum infrastructure is used to increase network connectivity and provide services such as interconnection. However, there is also the possibility of vehicles communicating via multiple hops. In vehicular networks, the *ad-hoc* mode is known as V2V *(Vehicle-to- Vehicle)* and the infrastructure mode is synonymous with the term V2I *(Vehicle-to-Infrastructure)*.

MANETs generally don't rely on any fixed infrastructure for communication and information dissemination. VANETs follow the same principle and apply it to the highly dynamic environment of surface transport.

VANETs can use fixed cellular gateways and WLAN access points at traffic intersections to connect to the Internet, collect traffic information or for routing purposes. The network architecture in this scenario is a purely cellular or WLAN structure, as shown in Figure 27. VANETs can combine cellular and WLAN to form the networks so that a WLAN is used where an access point is available or a 3G/4G connection otherwise. In addition, there are many studies for more modern networks and even for 5G technology applied in the future of next generation networks and the Internet of the Future.

Stationary or fixed gateways around the sides of roads could provide connectivity for mobile devices (vehicles), but are eventually impractical

Figure 27: Gateways/Routers in a Vehicular Network.

Source: (LI; WANG; CAROLINA, 2007)

considering the infrastructure costs involved. In this scenario, all the vehicles and wireless devices on a road can form a mobile *ad-hoc* network to carry out vehicle-to-vehicle communications and achieve certain objectives, such as blind intersection (an intersection without light control).

There is also a hybrid architecture that combines cellular, WLAN and *ad-hoc* networks and presents itself as a possible solution for VANETs. Namboodirt proposes such a hybrid architecture that uses some WLAN-capable vehicles and mobile phones as the mobile network gateways and routers so that WLAN-capable vehicles can communicate with them via multi-hop links to remain connected to the global backbone, the Internet.

VANETs comprise radio-enabled vehicles that act as mobile devices/nodes as well as routers for other devices/nodes. In addition to similarities with *ad-hoc* networks, such as radio transmission range, self-organisation and self-management and low bandwidth, VANETs can be distinguished from other types of *ad-hoc* networks by the following points:

- Highly dynamic topology: because the nodes in VANETs are vehicles, and because they move at high speed, the topology of VANETs changes frequently. There are already studies trying to find the approximate lifetime of a connection between vehicles;

- Frequently disconnected network: due to the dynamic nature of this type of network, the connectivity of VANETs also changes frequently, especially in environments with a low density of vehicles. In environments where there is a low vehicle density, the use of infrastructure architecture could be a solution to provide connectivity to the Internet, for example;

- Sufficient and stored energy capacity: the size of existing nodes, such as cars, buses, lorries, among others, makes it possible for them to have energy and the capacity to store and process information;

- Mobility modelling: The presence of buildings, trees, other vehicles and temperature conditions should be taken into account when communicating between nodes;

- Various communication environments: Mobility models should be considered in VANETs due to their unique mobility characteristics. Urban streets, roads or highways, buildings, trees, temperature conditions and other effects must be taken into account in VANETs, showing that the movement and communication of nodes is limited to these types of environments, and the behaviour of the driver at the wheel must also be taken into account, as they can react in different ways depending on the type of message they receive at the wheel.

The routing principle common to protocols used worldwide requires the presence of information on all available destinations in all the routers making up the network, in order to guarantee the delivery of traffic. As such, building large-scale networks using this routing principle is widely accepted as unscalable. The intrinsic problem with these mechanisms is that the routing tables keep pace with the growth of routing information in the network.

On the other hand, there are routing mechanisms available in the literature that require only a fraction of all the routing information present in the network, providing better control over the rate at which routing tables grow.

However, maintaining the coherence of this overlay network is challenging, since nodes can change their connection points in the network substrate, resulting in the use of different addresses (IPs) and requiring mechanisms to keep the association between the overlay network and the network substrate active.

4.3   Applicability

Road scenarios based on V2V communication are of particular interest for safety and therefore there are numerous valuable simulation studies on VANET performance in road scenarios.

Traffic in Brazil's big cities is increasingly congested. The increase in the number of vehicles, traffic accidents and road works have all contributed to impaired mobility in urban centres. Access to information about traffic conditions has therefore become an important part of the daily lives of Brazilians living in large and medium-sized cities across the country.

The use of information technology combined with telecommunications and electronics is a field of research aimed at developing systems for managing urban transport and communication between public transport managers and users.

Point-to-point multimedia content sharing (P2P) networking to multiple destinations has proven to be robust and highly scalable based on distributed solutions in the wired Internet. Significant research efforts are being put into extending P2P content delivery and its performance benefits to the wireless domain. Figure 28 outlines a vehicular scenario developed in the project.

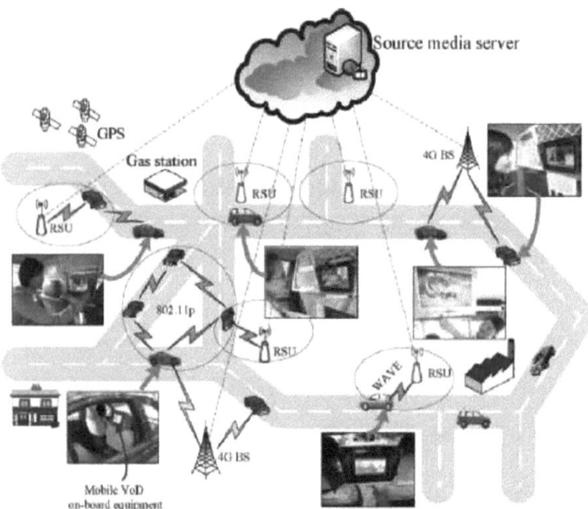

Figura 28:   System for Vehicular Networks.

Source: (LOBIYAL; KATTI; GIRI, 2015)

Lately, P2P-based multimedia services over vehicular *ad-hoc* networks (VANETs) have become very much a topic of research. However, despite growing attention from the research community, studies on P2P media delivery over VANETs have been limited to simple remote sequential playback scenarios, which are similar to broadcast mobile TV, where the passive user viewing pattern in relation to system design. However, user-centred mobile VoD services supporting interactivity can offer edited video clips to passengers on demand during their journeys, extending the services offered by YouTube fans, for example, from the office or home to the road. This represents one of the most innovative trends and value-added services in urban vehicles.

The area of study of routing is one of the most important in the concept of computer networks, as it is the crucial factor in determining whether a network protocol is good or bad, i.e. if the routing is excellent, then the network may well be too.

Routing is one of the main functions in computer networks and is responsible for routing traffic between pairs of source/destination nodes. Normally, the routing structure of a network is made up of a set of routers which, using a routing protocol, exchange information on the destinations available on the network to generate routing tables.

Based on these tables, traffic can be routed between nodes, and it is also the responsibility of the routing protocol to keep the routing tables up to date, representing the latest condition of the network after changes to its structure, in order to guarantee the delivery of traffic.

The routing protocols in most networks are organised into:

- Topology-based protocols make use of the principle that each node in the network maintains large-scale information about the network topology, the same principle that governs link-state-based routing protocols.

- Distance-based protocols do not maintain large-scale network topology information, but only the topology information needed to know the nearest neighbours.

- Distance-vector protocols, which maintain vectors of distances to each destination - the metric usually being the number of jumps.

- Basically, the routing principle of the protocols requires that the routers making up the network have information on all the available destinations in order to guarantee the correct delivery of traffic.

4.4   VANET evaluation through in-vehicle communications

For the study, an NS-3 simulator was used (NETWORK SIMULATOR 3, 2018), which already provides an implementation of the WAVE protocol suite that includes the IEEE 802.llp standard for the physical and MAC layers, and IEEE 1609 for the operations of the upper layers; in the physical layer, the biggest difference is the use of the 5.9 GHz band with a channel bandwidth of 10 MHz. These physical layer changes can make the wireless signal relatively more stable, without degrading data throughput.Table 3 shows the configuration of the parameters for the simulations carried out in this work. 2 vehicles were adopted to carry out V2V communication.

Table 3: Simulation parameters Scenario 1 VANET

Parameters	Values
Number of vehicles:	2
Delay model:	Constant Speed Propagation
Propagation model:	Two-Ray Ground
Height of antennae:	1.5 metres
MAC:	IEEE 802.llp WAVE

Linking nodes:	Ad-Hoc
Radio frequency:	5.9 GHz
Radio modulation:	OFDM 6Mbps BWlOMHz
Application of the coordinator node:	Eco Server
Transport protocol:	UDP
Type of traffic:	Continued
Packet size:	1024Mb (Megabit)
Simulation time:	300 Seconds

The IEEE 802.llp wireless communication standard for vehicular environments, where the radio has a frequency in the 5.9 Ghz range and uses the Direct-Sequence Spread Spectrum (DSSS) modulation technique, consists of a technique where the characteristics of the carrier (signal that is modulated) are modified in order to transmit the information, with combined changes being made to frequency, amplitude or phase (ROSS, 2010). Two propagation models were also adopted, Constant Speed Propagation to model delays and Two-Ray Ground (STOFFERS; RILEY, 2012) to model signal loss propagation. This radio propagation model predicts path losses between a transmitting antenna and a receiving antenna, and a height of 1.5 metres was assigned to the vehicle antennas to calculate the algorithm.

In order for a typical vehicular network to communicate, it is necessary to have a transport protocol that will govern the way in which packets are sent and received, data travels in the form of packets, the packet is a unitary data transmission structure, the information to be transmitted is generally broken down into numerous packets and then transmitted (ROSS, 2010; CATARINA et ah, 2009), for this simulation the UDP protocol (User Datagram Protocol) was used, further detail of these protocols is beyond the scope of this work. Having described the parameters for the communication channel, it now remains to describe the Echo Server application that will generate the network data flow: The application's Client vehicle is responsible for initiating communication as soon as the simulation starts, it will send packets with a size of 1024Mb (Megabit) to the Server vehicle, this vehicle waits to receive the packets from the Client vehicle, for each packet received the Server vehicle will echo (send) a packet of equal size to the originating Client vehicle, the type of traffic chosen was continuous (Constant Bit Rate) as realised in (OLIVEIRA; SALAZAR, 2014).Figure 29 describes the organisation of the scenarios and their mobility sets for V2V communications, the difference being predominantly in the speed of the vehicles

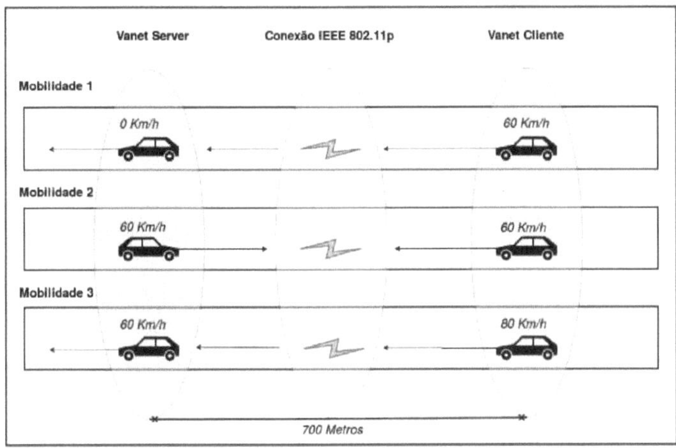

Figura 29:   Organisation of Scenario 1

Source: Author

In Mobility 1, the client vehicle is travelling at a constant speed of 60 km/h, and the server vehicle is travelling at 0 km/h. The main idea behind this mobility is to simulate a vehicle approach scenario, where we can understand that a vehicle is stopped at a traffic light, or parked on the edge of a motorway. Mobility 2 was intended to create a scenario where the two vehicles move at constant and equal speeds but in opposite directions. Mobility 3 describes a scenario where the server vehicle has a constant speed of 60 kilometres per hour and the client vehicle 80 kilometres per hour, with the aim of evaluating an approach scenario with two vehicles moving.

29.4.1   Results Scenario 1

Below are the graphs of the data collected in the NS-3 simulations using the *FlowMonitor* module (CATARINA et ah, 2009), which dynamically detects all the flows that pass through the network. The module also allows data flows to be evaluated in a paired manner by analysing just one set of nodes, which are made up of sender and receiver.

Figure 30 shows the data flow rate in V2V communication in the three mobility scenarios. The impact of vehicle speed on network performance is visible. It can be seen that in the scenarios where the relative speed between the vehicles was higher, the flow rate fell noticeably, for example in Mobility 1, where after 44 seconds of simulation the flow rate fell sharply, which was also influenced by the distance between the vehicles until it was no longer possible to receive data. In Mobility 3, on the other hand, the vehicles were travelling in the same direction, with the client travelling at a higher speed,

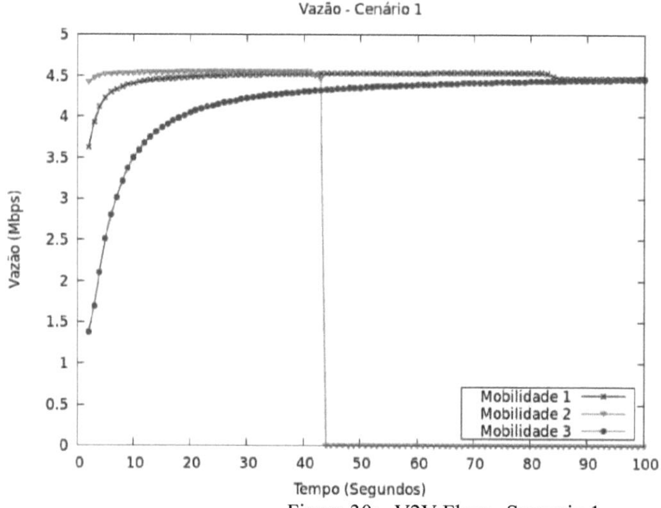

Figura 30:   V2V Flow - Scenario 1

Source: Author

the flow rate showed a slow increase until it reached peak values, once again influenced by distance.

Figure 31 shows the delay in V2V communication again in the three mobility scenarios. For this analysis, the closer the results are to zero, which means a network with fewer delays and better performance. Again, the stagnation of the results in Mobility 2 is noticeable after 44 seconds of simulation due to the disconnection of the vehicles caused by the distance. Mobility 3 had greater time variations than the other scenarios; the negative time results are caused by the loss of packets during transmission.

Figure 32 shows packet loss in V2V communication in the three mobility scenarios in question. For this analysis, the lower the loss, the better the network performance, it can be seen that Mobility 3 had a packet loss close to 60%, in second place was Mobility 1, which had a loss of approximately 19%, Mobility 3 had the best performance at around 9% loss, but this result can be considered doubtful, given that communication only takes place up to 44 seconds, after which time no more information is exchanged, so up to 44 seconds Mobility 3 had 9% packet loss.

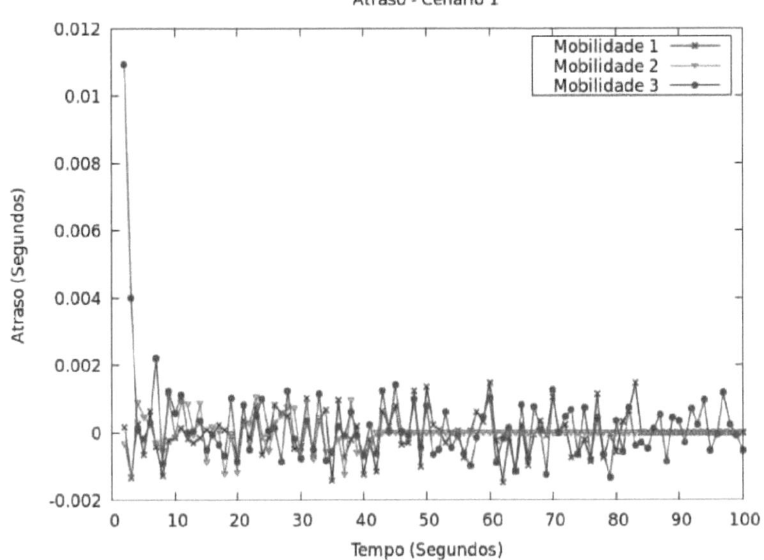

Figure 31: V2V delay - Scenario 1

Source: Author

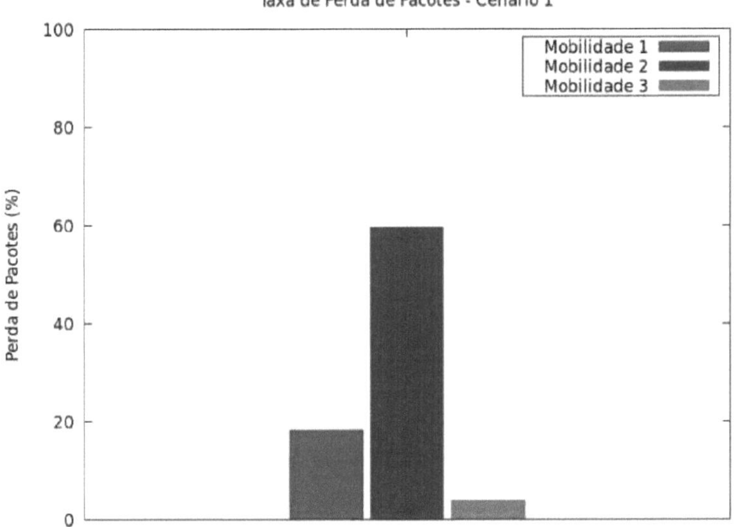

Figure 32: V2V delay - Scenario 1

Source: Author

4.5 Evaluating VANETs with a Realistic Mobility Model

0 second scenario reproduces the vehicle tracking files, its movement format is taken from (IST Lab, 2016). This scenario is a 300-second simulation with 99 vehicles distributed in the Unterstrass area of Zurich in Switzerland, the vehicles travelling based on models derived from real traffic data. In addition, three routing protocols were adopted AODV *(Ad-Hoc On-demand Distance Vector)* (TIWARI; KAUR, 2017), OLSR *(Optimised Link State Routing)* (STERNER; UPPMAN, 2017) and DSDV *(Destination Sequenced Distant Vector)* (DUGAEV et al., 2015). These protocols are widely used for various mobility applications that require high communication efficiency and low energy consumption, and the aim is to analyse the impact of changing the routing protocol on network performance.

Figure 33: Unterstrass area in Zurich, Switzerland

Source: (CONTRIBUTORS, 2012)

Figure 33 is exported from *OpenStreetMap*, which is a collaborative mapping project where it is possible to extract metrics to generate the mobility that will be used in the simulation.

Table 4 shows the configuration of parameters for the simulation of scenario 2, maintaining the same loss models adopted in scenario 1. The changes are in the number of vehicles, which for this scenario was 99. In addition, three routing protocols already used were adopted, AODV, OLSR and DSDV, which are responsible for routing the traffic generated by an application called OnOif native to the simulator in question. These applications use a data rate of 2048 bits per second with packets of 64 bytes in size.

Table 4: Simulation Parameters Scenario 2 VANET

Parameters	Values
Number of vehicles:	99
Delay model:	Constant Speed Propagation
Propagation model:	Two-Ray Ground

Height of antennae:	1.5 metres
MAC:	IEEE 802. llp WAVE
Linking nodes:	Ad-Hoc
Radio frequency:	5.9 GHz
Radio modulation:	OFDM 6Mbps BWlOMHz
Application of the coordinator node:	OnOíf
Transport protocol:	UDP
Routing protocols:	AODV, OLSR and DSDV
Data rate:	2048bps (bit per second)
Type of traffic:	Continued
Packet size:	64 Bytes
Simulation time:	300 Seconds

4.5.1   Results Scenario 2

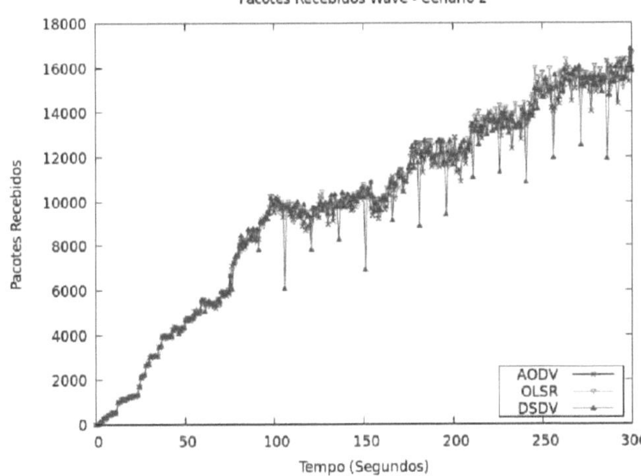

Figure 34: Comparison of Packets Received by Routing Protocol

Source: Author

Figure 34 shows the ratio of packets sent in simulation time for each of the routing protocols. The protocols show similar behaviour in terms of both increasing and decreasing actions, which can be explained by changes in mobility and network topology due to the route not being uniform. Even so, the DSDV protocol shows some drops compared to the others.

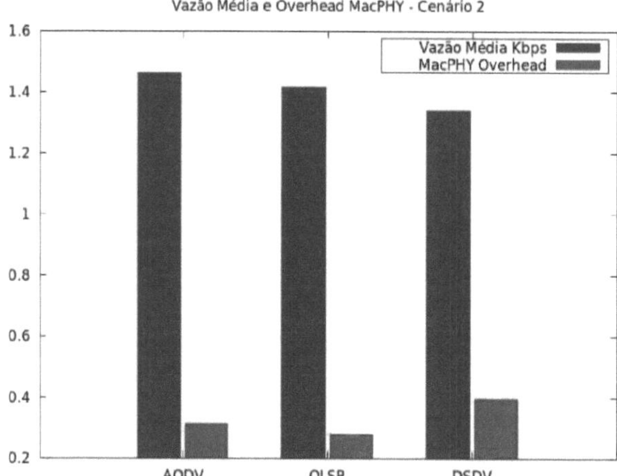

Figure 35: MAC/PHY Average Flow and Overhead Comparison

Source: Author

Figure 35 shows the average network throughput in relation to each routing protocol and also the Overhead results for the MAC and PHY layer, which were obtained by quantising the bytes generated by the WAVE model and the OnOff application. This metric is obtained from the difference between all WAVE bytes and all OnOff bytes and the result is divided again by the total number of WAVE bytes. Overhead is generally considered to be any excess processing or storage; for this evaluation, the higher the Overhead value means more bytes are generated in the communication. The AODV protocol had the highest average throughput compared to its competitors, while the DSDV protocol had the highest Overhead, which may be due to its proactive characteristic of periodically updating its routing table.

CHAPTER 5

Conclusions

The main objective of this research was to address new heterogeneous wireless architectures that can provide connectivity to users regardless of the type of technology and that can also support their transparent mobility.

To this end, the choice of protocols and technologies to be integrated to make up the new architectures is of paramount importance if the objective is to be achieved. The Fifth Generation will be a set of architectures with connectivity services. Current standards and technologies that can form this set include LTE technology, Mesh Networks and vehicular networks.

5G networks are getting closer to reality, although there are still many challenges for the new wireless network architectures.

Support for vertical mobility in heterogeneous scenarios is one of the requirements to be met, as it is necessary to guarantee support for quality of service for mobile users.

And support for vertical mobility management requires a set of techniques and algorithms capable of real-time monitoring of location, speed, type of application, signal strength, noise and other information needed to ensure that the user has quality connectivity regardless of the type of network they are connected to.

The large number of wireless networks available and the different types of services provided cause mobile devices to consume more battery power.

Although this research has not addressed any mechanism for saving battery energyconsumption, the choice of technology to be used can generate different energy consumption and this is a factor that can even be fundamental in decision-making.

There is a need for a balance between quality and energy consumption, as there will be times when the user opts for more quality and less battery life, just as there will be times when the user chooses to migrate to a network with less quality but more battery life.

The use of artificial intelligence techniques will be fundamental in mobile devices with multiple interfaces, since the change of technology will have to happen automatically without the user's influence.

Not least because the trend will be to add new technologies to the architecture to increase connectivity opportunities for mobile users.

Obviously there are still many challenges for 5G Networks, but it is also clear that it will bring a lot of improvements and change the concept of connectivity that exists today.

References

3GPP. 3GPP Release 8. 2008. Cited on page 13.

AKYILDIZ, I. F.; WANG, X.; WANG, W. Wireless mesh networks: a survey. *Computer Networks,* v. 47, n. 4, p. 445-487, 2005. ISSN 1389-1286. Available at: (http://www.sciencedirect.com/science/article/pii/S1389128604003457). Cited 4 times on pages 3, 27, 28 and 31.

ALVES, R. et al. An experimental analysis of the capacity of vehicular ad hoc networks. *XXVI SIMPÓSIO BRASILEIRO DE TELECOMUNICÇÕES SBrT2008,* p. 6, 2008. Cited on page 41.

ANAS, M. et al. Performance analysis of handover measurements and layer 3 filtering for UTRAN LTE. *IEEE International Symposium on Personal, Indoor and Mobile Radio Communications, PIMRC,* 2007. Cited on page 3.

AOYAMA, T. A new generation network: Beyond the internet and NGN. *IEEE Communications Magazine,* v. 47, n. 5, p. 82-87, 2009. ISSN 01636804. Cited twice on pages 1 and 7.

ASTELY, D. et al. LTE: the evolution of mobile broadband. *IEEE Communications magazine,* IEEE, v. 47, n. 4, 2009. Cited 3 times on pages 1, 3 and 12.

CATARINA, D. E. S. et al. Wireless sensor networks. *XXI Brazilian Symposium on Computer Networks,* 2009. Cited twice on pages 46 and 47.

CONNER, W. S. et al. IEEE 802.11 s Tutorial. *OverView of the Amendment for Wireless Local Area Mesh Networking. Intel Corp, Cisco Systems, TMicroelectronics, InterDigital Comm Corp,* 2006. Cited on page 30.

CONTRIBUTORS, O. Openstreetmap. *URL www. openstreetmap. org,* 2012. Quoted on page 50.

D'AVILA, C. K. Tutorial: LTE: Long Term Evolution - Basic Architecture and Multiple Access. *CEDET - Centre for Professional and Technological Development,* p. 1-8, 2009. Available at: (http://www.cedet.com.br/index.php7/Tutoriais/Telecom/ lte-long-term-evolution-basic-architecture-and-multiple-access.html). Quoted on page 8.

DHIMAN, A.; SANDHA, K. S. *Vertical and Horizontal Handover in Heterogeneous Wireless Networks.* 1-76 p. Thesis (PhD) - Thapar University, 2013. Available at: (http://hdl.handle.net/10266/2361). Cited on page 13.

DUGAEV, D. et al. A survey and performance evaluation of ad-hoc multi-hop routing protocols for static outdoor networks. *2015 International Siberian Conference on Control and Communications, SIBCON 2015 - Proceedings,* 2015. Cited on page 50.

ET, E. D. *fG LTE-Advanced for Mobile Broadband.* [S.I.: s.n.], 2011. 1-5 p. ISSN 0717-6163. ISBN 9780874216561. Cited on page 1.

ETSI. *Transportation.* 2018. Available at: (https://www.etsi.org/technologies-clusters/ clusters/transportation). Quoted on page 40.

IST Lab. *Realistic Vehicular Traces.* 2016. Available at: (http://www.lst.inf.ethz.ch/ research/ad-hoc/car-traces/). Cited on page 50.

KADAH, N. A.; NOLL, J. *Mobility & Handover in mobile systems*. 2012. Available at: (http://its-wiki.nO/images/9/9a/Basics_Handover.pdf). Quoted on page 14.

KHAN, J. Handover management in GSM cellular system. *International Journal of Computer Applications*, v. 8, n. 12, p. 14-24, 2010. Cited on page 13.

LI, F.; WANG, Y.; CAROLINA, N. Routing in Vehicular Ad Hoc Networks : A Survey. *IEEE Vehicular Technology Magazine*, n. June, p. 12-22, 2007. ISSN 1556-6072. Cited twice on pages 38 and 42.

LOBIYAL, D. K.; KATTI, C. P.; GIRI, A. K. Parameter value optimization of ad-hoc on demand multipath distance vector routing using particle swarm optimization. *Procedia Computer Science*, v. 46, p. 151-158, 2015. ISSN 18770509. Cited on page 44.

MESHNET, U. *UCSB MeshNet*. 2007. Available at: (http://moment.cs.ucsb.edu/ meshnet/). Quoted on page 2.

MOHR, D. et al. Automotive revolution - perspective towards 2030. How the convergence of disruptive technology-driven trends could transform the auto industry. *McKinsey & Company*, v. 5, n. 4, p. 20-25, 2016. ISSN 2250-3390. Disponível em: (http://link.springer.com/10.1365/s40112-016-1117-8). Quoted on page 4.

NETWORK SIMULATOR 3. *Release ns-3.25*. 2016. Available at: (https: //www.nsnam.org/ns-3-25/). Cited 3 times on pages 5, 8 and 11.

NETWORK SIMULATOR 3. *PropagationLossModel Class Reference*. 2018. Available at: (https://www.nsnam.org/doxygen/group__propagation.html). Cited on page 45.

OLIVEIRA, F. D. M.; SALAZAR, A. O. QoS Analysis of Routing Protocols in Wireless Sensor Networks in the Monitoring of Wind Farms. 2014. Cited on page 46.

PAIER, A. et al. Car-to-car radio channel measurements at 5 GHz: Pathloss, power delay proile, and Doppler delay spectra. *Proc. Jth Int. Symp. on Wireless Communication Systems, ISWCS'07*, p. 224-228, 2007. Cited on page 39.

REICHARDT, D. et al. CarTALK 2000: safe and comfortable driving based upon inter-vehicle-communication. *Intelligent Vehicle Symposium, 2002. IEEE*, v. 2, p. 545-550, 2002. Available at: (http://ieeexplore.ieee.org/lpdocs/epic03/wrapper.htm? arnumber=1188007). Quoted on page 38.

RICARDO, C. A. *Optimisation of the Vertical Handover Decision Process in Networks Based on the IP Multimedia Subsystem (IMS)*. Thesis (Master's Degree in Applied Informatics) - Pontifical Catholic University, 2009. Cited twice on pages 13 and 14.

ROSS, K. Computer Networks and the Internet, p. 618, 2010. Quoted on page 46.

SALES, D. F. *Analysis of inter- and intra-cell Handover in a Mobile Phone System using a Simplified Measurement Method*. Thesis (Master's Dissertation in Electrical and Computer Engineering) - Federal University of Rio Grande do Norte, 2009. Cited on page 13.

SIQUEIRA, G. L. *Coexistence between 3 and 4 Generation Technologies*. Thesis (Doctorate) - PUC-Rio, 2011. Available at: (https://www.maxwell.vrac.puc-rio.br/18484/ 18484_3.PDF). Cited on page 12.

STERNER, U.; UPPMAN, U. On the robustness of OLSR in a mobile tactical scenario in rural terrain. *2017 International Conference on Military Communications and Information Systems, ICMCIS 2017,* 2017. Cited on page 50.

STOFFERS, M.; RILEY, G. Comparing the ns - 3 Propagation Models. *Modelling, Analysis & Simulation of Computer and Telecommunication Systems (MASCOTS),* p. 61-67, 2012. Cited on page 46.

TALIWAL, V. et al. Empirical determination of channel characteristics for DSRC vehicle-to-vehicle communication. *Proceedings of the first ACM workshop on Vehicular ad hoc networks - VANET '04,* p. 88, 2004. Available at: (http: //portal.acm.org/citation.cfm?doid=1023875.1023890). Quoted on page 39.

TANENBAW, A. S.; DAVID, W. *Computer Networks.* 5. ed. [S.l.]: Pearson, 2011. 586 p. ISBN 9788576059240. Cited on page 15.

TELECO. *FG coverage in Brazil.* 2018. Available at: (http://www.teleco.com.br/ 4g_cobertura.asp). Quoted on page 7.

TELECO. *LTE: Network Concepts.* 2018. Available at: (http://www.teleco.com.br/ tutorials/tutorialintlte/pagina_4.asp). Quoted on page 9.

TIWARI, A.; KAUR, I. Performance Evaluation of Energy Efficient For MANET Using AODV Routing Protocol. *3rd IEEE International Conference on "Computational Intelligence and Communication Technology"(IEEE-CICT 2017),* p. 1-5, 2017. Cited on page 50.

YAQOOB, I. et al. Overcoming the key challenges to establishing vehicular communication: Is SDN the answer? *IEEE Communications Magazine,* v. 55, n. 7, p. 128-135, 2017. ISSN 01636804. Cited twice on pages 3 and 4.

ZHANG, H.; BAI, F.; JU, X. Heterogeneous vehicular wireless networking: A theoretical perspective. *2015 IEEE Wireless Communications and Networking Conference, WCNC 2015,* p. 1936-1941, 2015. Cited on page 4.

I want morebooks!

Buy your books fast and straightforward online - at one of world's fastest growing online book stores! Environmentally sound due to Print-on-Demand technologies.

Buy your books online at
www.morebooks.shop

Kaufen Sie Ihre Bücher schnell und unkompliziert online – auf einer der am schnellsten wachsenden Buchhandelsplattformen weltweit! Dank Print-On-Demand umwelt- und ressourcenschonend produziert.

Bücher schneller online kaufen
www.morebooks.shop

Printed by Books on Demand GmbH, Norderstedt / Germany